A MYTH IN ACTION:
THE HEROIC LIFE OF AUDIE MURPHY

A MYTH IN ACTION:
The Heroic Life of Audie Murphy
(A comparison of the life of Audie Murphy to the typical lives of mythological hero figures.)

by

Ann Levingston Joiner
(copyright 1998)
Published by Middle of the Forest Press
All rights reserved; no part of this book may be reproduced, stored in a retrieval system or transmitted in any form or by any means, electronic, mechanical, photocopying or otherwise, without the prior written permission of the publisher.

A Myth in Action:
The Heroic Life of Audie Murphy
Table of Contents

Preface 9

The Myth
"Ode to a Lost Warrior" 15

Introduction 27

1 Primordial Background 37
2 The Hero as Warrior 41
3 The Childhood of the Mythological Hero 43
4 The Childhood of Audie Murphy 47

BOOK I – The Hero's Journey

Part 1 – Separation 57
1 The Call to Adventure
2 Supernatural Aid 59
3 Crossing the First Threshold 63
4 The Belly of the Whale 67

Part 2 – Initiation
(The Dark Side of the Journey)

The Road of Trials
1 Sicily: The Lesson of Reality   71
2 Salerno to the Mignano Gap: The Lesson of Irony   85
3 Naples: The Meeting with the Goddess   97
4 Anzio: The Lesson of Futility   101
5 France: The Nadir of the Journey   119
The Landing at Ramatuelle
Montelimar (The Face in the Mirror)
The Vosges Mountains
6 Apotheosis   139
7 The Granting of the Boon   147

Part 3 – The Return
San Antonio to Farmersville   151
The Wound that Would Not Heal

BOOK II
Delivering the Message

Introduction
1 Stranger in a Strange Land   175
2 Bad Boy of Hollywood   187
3 Master of Two Worlds   193
4 From "Duel" to "Destry"   201
The Camelot Years:
Retelling the Arthurian Legend Onscreen
5 Reliving Hell   215
6 Fatherhood   219
The Hero as Emperor and/or Tyrant
7 The Freedom to Live   225
8 Songwriter   239

9 The Last Real Action Hero   243
10 Departure   251

BIBLIOGRAPHY

ENDNOTES

A MYTH IN ACTION:
The Heroic Life of Audie Murphy

Preface

The year was 1953. I sat in an old movie theater, clutching my bag of popcorn, watching a young man astride a gangly nag of a horse climb a Technicolor cliff. Near the top, the young man turned to look behind him and saw the sheriff who had been chasing him fall onto a dry water hole. The young man knew, as we in the audience knew, that without help, the sheriff would soon die of thirst. The young man looked ahead again, to his freedom and the chance to prove he was innocent of the charges that had led to this chase, hesitated, and finally saying, "I just ain't got the sense I was born with," returned to the dry hole and saved the sheriff, putting his own future in jeopardy. In doing so, he stumbled onto a solution that would not only save himself, but also lead to a "treasure" that would restore prosperity to his whole community, and, of course, he got the girl. In those moments in that dark theater, my own personal concept of the term "hero" was born. I was ten years old. The name of the movie was "Tumbleweed." The actor's name was Audie Murphy. Over the next two years, I would see every movie he made. That was easy enough to do, for every Saturday during those years, my mother would send me off to that neighborhood theater with my older brother, each of us clutching a fifty-cent piece. One quarter each got us in; the other kept us in popcorn, sugary candies, and soft drinks, which lasted us from the cartoons, through the serials, to the double-feature westerns at the end. I liked Westerns generally, but the two or three times a year that they would star Audie Murphy, I was ecstatic.

Then, in 1955, he made a movie called "To Hell and Back." I did not go to see this one; it was a war movie, and I didn't care much for war movies. My older brother saw it, and talked about it for days. I caught from my brother that it was a true story, and that Audie Murphy had played himself, that he had been a real hero before he began playing them in the movies, and I thought that was nice, but continued to prefer seeing him in western roles.

In 1957, he made a movie with Jimmy Stewart, and played a "bad guy," and died at the end of the movie. I went home and stayed up all night, rewriting the movie so that he was "good," and lived on at the end, "happily ever after." This was the hero concept I still wanted to see. By this time, I was dating, and my childhood hero fantasies began to fade. I do remember in 1960, looking through my American History textbook, and seeing a familiar grinning face in a picture: a young boy covered with medals. Sure enough, the caption identified the boy as Audie Murphy, the most decorated soldier of W.W.II, but for the most part, Audie Murphy slipped back into the corners of my memory. And after the beginnings of the war in Vietnam, I found myself consciously rejecting him. At that time, I had still not seen his autobiographical film, "To Hell and Back." I was a rather non-aggressive person, and was appalled over America's entry into that war. I could no longer ignore Murphy's warrior roots. It was even said that GI's in Vietnam referred to the most gung-ho of their brothers as "real Audie Murphys." I recall a day in 1971, while I was pregnant with my third child, reading a small entry at the back of the local newspaper, saying that Audie Murphy had died in a plane crash, briefly stating that the former war hero had died penniless. It disturbed and saddened me momentarily, but I put that, too, in the back corner of my mind, and continued to live a life that "happened," as the saying goes, while I was making other plans.

In 1977, close to a quarter of a century after that first film, while in the process of getting a divorce, I sat with my own children in the same theater, once again clutching a bag of popcorn, as the screen caption rolled by: "A long time ago, in a galaxy far, far away...." The setting had changed from six-shooters and horses to space ships and light sabers, and the production was much slicker, but the basic story was the same. After years of "Midnight Cowboy"'s and "French Connection"'s, the movies had returned to the themes I had grown up with. Even before I was old enough to go with my brother to that theater, and having learned to read at a very early age, I would escape to the easy chair in the corner of my room and retreat into a world of fairy tales and adventures. My two favorite books were beautiful leather-bound and intricately illustrated volumes: *Fairy Tales from Hans Christian Anderson and Household Tales* by Jacob and Wilhelm Grimm. I devoured every story, but my favorite character, the one I most identified with, was Snow White. My father was a dear, gentle, and very kind man, but he never had the courage to stand up to my mother, even when her actions were detrimental to my brothers or to me. Perhaps as a consequence, the part of me that a Jungian analyst would call my *animus* was rather weak. Like Snow White, I was perfectly lady-like, but completely helpless when it was time for me to stand up for myself. I believe that is why I became so enthralled with western movies and made heroes of cowboys and frontier lawmen. I had especially liked the personae adopted by Audie Murphy, because like my father, they were invariably slight, as my father was, and quiet and gentle, like my father was, always preferring to find a non-violent solution to a problem, but unlike my father, whenever any injustice occurred, they accepted the responsibility for setting things right, often defeating tyrants who were twice their size. So at that first moment when Luke Skywalker picked up and brandished his father's lightsaber, I, along with my children, became a fanatic, and the reassurances from many such movies over the next few years would help me build the courage to move my children westward a hundred miles to the city of Houston, where I began a new life as an English teacher.

    The return of Romantic themes to the movies led me back to my interest in Romantic Literature, and the stories of legend and myth. I found a certain comfort in the recurring themes and timeless plots. They provided me with a basis for developing the set of beliefs I would shape my life with. Frequently, I used mythology and mythological stories as a means of providing the continuity my students needed to make the connections that allowed them to grasp higher-order thinking concepts. Joseph Campbell's "Hero Cycle," archetypal literary analysis, and even the early *Star Wars* film plots all made their way into my classrooms. But by the early '90's, my children had all grown up and left home, and the vacant spaces left a void inside me that I had a difficult time trying to fill. My mother died a few years later, and I went through a year of feeling almost nothing, until one summer day, while I was on break from my teaching job, I happened to notice, thumbing through my TV programming guide, that June 20 was Audie Murphy's birthday, and that American Movie Classics was honoring him with a whole day of his movies. I felt excitement for the first time in a long year, and spent the day reliving a childhood of hope and dreams. It might have remained just a pleasant day had I not noticed, a few days later, that A&E Biography was planning to show the story of his life during the week of Independence Day. I watched, and for the whole hour, sat enthralled. Here was a real human being; flawed, like the rest of us, whose life and death took on mythological proportions, but was, at the same time, recent enough not to have been embellished or distorted. Audie Murphy was neither the fairy-tale knight of his movies, nor the gung-ho glory-seeking warrior that he was perceived to be during the late Sixties. He was much more. There was something quite profound to this man that the hour-long biography merely hinted at. I wanted to know more, and so, I began my own quest, to find the man behind the movie personae, the medals, and the media. The following pages relate the result of that quest.

The Myth

Ode to a Lost Warrior:
by
Ann Levingston Joiner

The Beginnings

Another dying warrior stands defiant,
Hundreds of withered arms each ending
in five gnarled fingers
    clinging tenaciously
to the final products of its life
    (perhaps remembering green youth and
the too-rapid loss
    of briefly white, then red and
bleeding petals)

No match for the battling boy whose
    nimble fingers deftly pluck away the
        tightly clutched tufts,
dropping them into the canvas sack
    several times longer than the boy is tall.

Ignoring his own trepidation,
he boldly peers down long rows
    of similar dying warriors - their
        fibrous balls waiting mutely

for him in the Texas sun.

The endless spheres of white
take on a cloud-like haze as the boy
        dreams of greater battles yet to come.
More formidable enemies - worthy opponents
to overcome with greater honor.
        (In his pocket lies heavily
    one tiny brazen shell
    to be put to use when this day's
    work is done.)

The long sack finally bulging the boy
turns it over to be weighed
        and takes his meager wages - too little
            to buy food,
and so picks up the rifle and
loading it with the single shell
heads to a world more friendly and inviting.

In the woods, alone, moving silently,
    feeling
    finally at home - one with the
shimmering late-day beauty
    sharp ears detect a rustle
        of leaves overhead - sharp eyes a flick
            of bushy tail - the gun swung up
                deftly, one shot and it is
done.
The single shell hit home. He claims the prize
which means one night less hungry.

The gnawing lessened in their bellies he puts
his brothers and sisters to bed and
                returns to the chair
      where his mother sits, long
chestnut hair released, hands still in
        her lap, twisted, cramped fingers
              aching again from too much use.

The boy kneads them gently, desperately
watching
her face for response, seeing only a
        vacant stare from a heart
grown cold from too little love, too much work,
and too many children,
            feeling only relief.
The abusive man they call husband and
father is once again absent. Not until the
boy has gone down to a restless sleep does
        she picks up his one pair of
            cast-off overalls and wash them,
                leaving them to dry by the
stove for morning.

The denim, faded and frayed from
      too many washings has drawn
      the trousers even shorter.
The boy, seeing his bare ankles
envisions the coming derision
        and perceives grimly that
            there will be more fights this day.

The teacher watches him arrive - his reddish hair
    and freckled face washed shining clean.
As he moves quickly to his desk,
    she resists asking of his absences,
    again so many days. His classmates watch.
 A curious mix of disdain and admiration.
Among the boys
    willing to risk their parents displeasure,
    he has his followers
but the chestnut-haired girl in starched linen
    sits scornfully in front of him.

Inside his desk, his one reprieve.
He lifts and gently fingers the books - escaping to
    a distant world of hope and dreams
    and full bellies.

But even in this joy - a sadness lurks. Already
    he knows the limit to these days. This respite, too brief.
 His mother and the other children are
    too hungry - his useless father gone longer
    and longer periods of time.

The Adventure

The boy-man crouches
>	in the wet, muddy foxhole, listening
>	to the incessant wind mixed with
>>	the sounds of exploding shells.

At night, his dreams intermingle scenes: stark
white fields of cotton, his mother's early
>	but solacing death,
>	stalking this formidable
>>	enemy with one shell in his gun.

Trading the foxhole to crouch in the now-familiar
>	whale-like belly of the landing craft -
"I hope I get to see France," he wrote to a
friend. Approaching the shore,
>	remembering, he laughs,
>>	almost hysterically.

Ashore, amid the whistling and exploding
>	shells echoes the rat-tat of the machine
gun.
The men who follow him look
>	to him with eyes like the defiant school-boys
>>	of that long-ago time.

The gun must not be met head-on. Choosing a
safe,
>	circuitous route, he goes out
>	alone - but not quite alone -
>>	followed by his closest friend who

     refuses to go back. The gun
    burps out again
      his friend falls. (A letter
from his
   daughter in his pocket: "Deer Daddy, I
am in school")
Remembering the too-little time he spent in
school
    he pictures the child, in class with
      her spelling lessons, oblivious
      to the fact that she is suddenly
fatherless.

Rage wells up, finally - his
    too few school days, his mother's eyes
      as vacant while half-alive as his
       now-dead friend in his arms.

He charges the hill, seeing
in the face of every enemy the face of
   his own too-absent father.
(If the only escape with honor was in a body
bag
he could at least go home with his friend.)
At length he stands alone upon the hill,
   alive. The enemy lying dead around him.
Returning to his friend he sheds his last tears.

The house stood dark with shadows and the
    smell of death and he knew the enemy
    still lurked in darkened places. When

the evil creature with
his father's face and glaring
      blood-shot eyes appeared, he fired at
once.
In the shattering slivered glass he saw
      the disintegration of
           his own reflection.
(His buddies joked about a Texan
      beating himself to the draw.)

Stalking through the forest, the
      new brass bars he did not want burning
      into his shoulders, weighing them
           even more heavily, he heard a rifle
crack
      finally felt the searing pain that even
           in its intensity came as relief.

Cool sheets and the woman in
white with chestnut hair - a temporary reprieve
-
      "Next time," he wrote home, "I
guess
           they'll tag me for keeps."

Too soon back at the front the orders
come through: "Hold the road at all costs."
      (the cost already having taken
      four-fifths of the one hundred-plus men
      under his command. Their only support

        two useless tanks, one already in flames.)

Those left looked to him with eyes
      too much like siblings and school boys so that
      when he saw the enemy - over two hundred
strong with six lumbering tanks approaching -
ten times outnumbered, the phone he used
      to call in distant artillery not enough - he jumped
upon the useless burning tank,
      shoving bodies aside,
      ignoring "smell of burning flesh"
to fire the tank's machine gun, raking
      repeatedly the approaching enemy - next time
      they'll get me for keeps and body bags
      the only honorable escape and so mr. artillery man
        what are your post war plans?

Surprised to find himself alive as the enemy
      retreats, the boy-warrior
      gathers up his men....

Coming Home

Back in the glaring Texas sun
    the plane lands. Beneath him
    are crowds cheering and he
        flinches at artillery salutes and
        cringes at endless speeches. The medals
on his chest already an albatross - he endured the shame
    of being sent home a living trophy to the
    blood and death of too many friends.

Unknowingly become an ICON, the
    man-boy-soldier with too little schooling soon
        found himself in a celluloid world of too much
    light and too many happy endings: Too many people
        clamoring to touch him.

With the praise and
    applause came the tiny
    chestnut-haired women, the second giving him the only prize he
truly valued - two healthy sons who would never
    know hunger or the pain felt and rage directed at
        a father whose absence at least meant
        the absence of brutality.

(Later he would speak of animals and
children as the only all-good creatures left.)

Too often he lived in a
too-light make-believe world of good
      always defeating evil
          from which he reconciled himself with
              "It beats pickin' cotton,"
and knowledge that he at least gave
children hope of making a better world.

But sometimes
at night, escaping the still persistent dreams
      of blood and battle and dying buddies
        he would find himself in too-dark places.
Places where he saw other fathers - fathers
      with pock-marked arms and such
powerful syringes
        the men left their daughters to
          play in the dirt and their
wives to
        sell themselves. Here was
another war
more terrible in its hopelessness - a war
      he fought in the dark while
        in the daylight hours he gave children
          joy and hope in happy endings as
he found what
        joy and hope he could in his two
growing sons and
the too few distant friends which he kept

  at bay because he could not bear more
losses.

But a time came when even the
celluloid-world-where-good-guys-always-win-
and-only-villains-die
  was fading - fading
    as the world was changing
    as wars and threats of wars
continued in
the real-life world. Working with the
  make-believe he journeyed to
    a land where
children with yellow skin and black
  eyes which looked strangely like the eyes
    of his brothers and sisters
    (and now his own sons) - children
who
were losing their fathers in a war - a war
  that would soon see still more
    young warrior-fathers from his own land
      die or come home maimed and
fated to wake screaming
from the same dreams he still
  waked from.

Still he fought to keep alive
a much-needed vision:
  a world of light and hope for his own
children
  and the growing number of fatherless
children.

This vision took him on
        a mission - and a small plane
        carried him to his final
                destiny with a Virginia
mountainside - a destiny
which finally tagged him for keeps.

Our memories of the boy-warrior-man
        too quickly fade.
After a too-long time
        we finally begin to remember.

A MYTH IN ACTION:
The Heroic Life of Audie Murphy

INTRODUCTION

> "There is one story and one story only
> That will prove worth your telling..."
> Robert Graves

The stories of Jim Harvey of "Tumbleweed," Luke Skywalker of the *Star Wars* saga, and Audie Murphy are all versions of the same story, a tale that has been told and retold from our prehistoric beginnings, across every culture. It is the story of the mythological hero. These heroic legends all share the same basic structure, one that wells up from our unconscious, and one that we recognize and respond to most strongly when we have the most need for its retelling. Rollo May asserts that the hero symbolizes "the highest aims of the community,"[2] as he explains how, "Heroes are necessary in order to enable the citizens to find their own ideals, courage, and wisdom in the society.... We hunger for heroes," he continues, "as role models, as standards of action, as ethics in flesh and bones like our own. *A hero is a myth in action*."[3]

The plot structure of the typical hero's tale follows the outlines explored by Joseph Campbell, in his book, *The Hero with a Thousand Faces*.[4] Campbell explains how the story invariably begins with a young man who has a strong compulsion to leave home. He may not answer this "call" right away, especially if his home is a happy one. Sooner or later, though, armed with gifts and "amulets" provided by his "helpers," sometimes older men and/or women, sometimes friendly animals, "with whom he has a mystical rapport," he sets out. He may wander for a while, but he eventually comes to a threshold, where he must fight his first battle, to prove he is worthy to enter the "dark kingdom." This "kingdom" may be a dark forest, a desert wasteland, or a night sea-journey. If he wins the battle with the guardian of the threshold, he enters a place of darkness where he must withstand several preliminary trials before he reaches the nadir, or darkest point of the journey. The "amulets" and gifts from earlier helpers are put to use, and she often meets more helpers during this "road of trials." There at this darkest part of the journey the hero must conquer an evil force, a tyrant or dragon. If his meeting with this dark force is successful, she is given a "boon," a treasure, magic elixir, or a truth, each of which represents life, and is allowed to return home. If the hero has not killed or appeased the dark force, he may have to steal the treasure and flee for his life like Jack the Giant-Killer in the beanstalk tale. At any rate, it is his duty to return home and share the "boon" with family and neighbors in order to restore prosperity to the homeland. The journey is always a circular one, enabling the hero to, in the words of T. S. Eliot, "arrive at the place where [he] started, and know the place for the first time."[5] Various researchers have extensively studied the plot structure of the hero tale as it appears in myth, legend, fairy tale, and Romance. While these individuals used different terminology, they invariably found the same elements and sequence. Jole Cappiello McCurdy refers to Vladimir Propp's study of the structure of the fairy tale, and to Propp's 31 separate steps of the hero's journey.[6] While Propp's list is more detailed, the sequence is the same as Campbell's. Step 1 explains the conditions that will lead to the hero leaving home. In Step 12, he or she meets a "donor," who will provide the magical aids that will help to overcome the trials. In Step 15, the hero reaches what Campbell calls the "nadir" of the journey, the place, often a castle, "where the main deeds will take place."[7] The "villain is defeated" in Step 18, She "returns home" in Step 20. Steps 21 through 31 refer to the period immediately following that return. Propp's study was limited to fairy tales, but McCurdy also notes similar studies by Claude Levi-

Strauss and Marie-Louise von Franz who find the same cycles in myth.[8]

In whatever time and place it appears, a myth has the same source as our dreams.[9] Both rise out of our "collective unconscious" in the form of "archetypes," or symbolic patterns of stories, characters, and themes;[10] to point the way to a better life; and they appear when there is a need to change, to leave the old life behind and begin the journey to a new one. While a dream speaks to the individual, a myth speaks to the whole community. According to Rollo May, "Myths are the narrative patterns that give significance to our existence."[11] A community's myths force it to see life in a different way. This "new" way of seeing things is often simply a return to an older way, which has been lost somehow, causing us to live inauthentic lives, creating a "wasteland" of infertility and stagnation, and a sense of alienation. In every society, the old myths eventually become covered over with the visions of the society's authority, or are taken to be literal truths rather than symbolic ones. At this point, a new hero must appear, to rediscover the underlying truth, and guide us toward putting aside the inauthentic values we have adopted.[12] People need these heroes. Without their guidance and examples, we flounder, unable to choose suitable responses and our community becomes a part of the growing wasteland.

Our 21st century life is so fast-paced that people, especially young people, often have trouble seeing the relevance of the heroic efforts of those who lived hundreds or thousands of years ago. But Audie Murphy's life story provides us with a modern hero, a man of our time, a man who, as May says, "reflects our own sense of identity, our combined emotions, our myths."[13] And a major difference between the story of Audie Murphy and the stories of myth and legend is that Audie Murphy's story is true. He lived recently enough for his life to be researched and documented. But the significance of his life is not merely that it can be proven, for it also validates the underlying myth and its message; therefore it indicates that any one of us can become a hero.

The hero story is not only told in our myths, it is repeated in our movies, our fairy tales, legends, and romantic fiction. According to psychotherapist Stephen Flynn, "Whatever stance one takes either with religion, myth, or fairy tale, they all share a common purpose of transmitting meaning. Both fairy tale and myth ...contain an underlying pattern that speaks to our present day condition."[14] That "underlying pattern" gives the same psychological significance to lighter stories, like those we find in fairy tales, Romantic fiction, and film, as that found in myth and religion. Yet, while there is a clear and obvious connection between myth and legend on the one hand and fairy tales and light Romantic fiction on the other, light Romance and fairy tales often end "happily ever after." But myth and legend, like the archetypal sources they spring from, almost never end "happily ever after." These stories go beyond the adventure to tell how the hero returns home to great acclaim, but eventually "loses favor,"[15] and the myths and legends let us know that the message of the hero's return is frequently ignored by the very people it was intended to save.[16] Sometimes, the hero is even made a scapegoat, and sent out into the wilderness, carrying the sins of the people with him, so that they are free to go on living as they choose, rather than as they ought.[17]

Carol Pearson, in her book, *The Hero Within*, speaks of six archetypes that influence the life of the hero during different stages. First, in early childhood, the hero is an "Innocent," who believes completely that the world is a place of safety and comfort. Sooner or later, the child becomes an "Orphan," so-called because he or she has learned that even parents cannot always be trusted as protectors. Pearson refers to leaving home as the beginning of the archetypal influence of the "Wanderer," at which point the hero responds to the "Call to Adventure" spoken of by Campbell. She elaborates on the basic structure by pointing out that the next two phases often differ for men and women. For most men, the next stage is that of the

"Warrior," whose job is to "defeat the enemy," while women most often at this point enter the stage of the "Martyr," whose job is one of "sacrificing self for others." Women usually enter the "Warrioring" stage during maturity, while men, at that phase of their lives, become "Martyrs." She describes the difference between "Warrioring" and "Martyring" by saying that, "Warriors strive to be strong, to have an imprint on the world, and to avoid ineffectiveness and passivity," while, "Martyrs," on the other hand, "want to be good, and see the world as a conflict between good (care and responsibility), and bad (selfishness and exploitation.)" Eventually, the hero becomes a "Magician," sometimes referred to as a "Shaman." At this stage the hero is able to see, through his or her own inner wisdom, the rightness of the universe. There are similarities to the worldviews of the "Magician" and the "Innocent," but the "Magician" has taken the hero's journey and returned. The "Innocent" has never left. Pearson differs, too from other researchers in that she does not rely on sequence as strongly as the other experts do. She insists that all of the archetypes are present and at work all of the time, and that the stages frequently overlap.[18]

In our own time, especially during the last thirty years, we have attempted to deny the reality of the archetypal "warrior" hero, because of our knowledge of the total devastation another major war would bring. War in our time is a terrible and fearsome happening, but rejection and repression of the warrior archetype, which is a psychological reality within each of our own minds, will not eliminate war. Repressing the aggressive side of human nature doesn't get rid of it. It is merely removed to what Carl Jung called our "Shadow," the parts of our personalities we don't want to see or have recognized. Refusing to accept our Shadow qualities may very well cause us to externalize our aggression and project it onto others. Refusing to admit that as humans we are naturally aggressive creatures might also prevent us from recognizing the danger from outside our own communities when it is present. The warrior must be remembered, upheld as an essential part of our selves and our culture, and returned to a place of honor, if we are to survive.

"In the profound sense," says Rollo May, "the hero is created by us as we identify with the deeds he or she performs."[19] Out of a psychic knowledge of our need for this hero, we envision not only his life, but his mysterious death as well. The places of his death and his burial, as well as the place of his birth, become hallowed ground.[20] We begin to long for his return, even for his rebirth. During the last few years, Audie Murphy's life, his movies, and his message are being remembered. Audie Murphy is being "reborn." Perhaps it is because at this critical point, the end and the beginning of a millennium, we need him more than ever.

To understand the heroism of Audie Murphy, we need to look, not only at his heroic deeds, but at the life he lived both before and after his journey "to hell and back," to recognize that his whole life falls in line with the lives of those heroes of myth. Facing the trials of a new millennium, we need, finally, to hear his message, and heed it. All of us carry the archetype of the "warrior" within us. It is this archetype that gives us courage, and helps us to fight when fighting is necessary. We are currently living in a wasteland of alienation and violence, when the old answers don't work. If we are to survive, we need to honor all of the archetypes of our unconsciousness, including the warrior, and we need to remember and honor the men and women who represent them. As May points out in *The Cry for Myth*, "The rediscovery of heroism is central in the regaining of our myths and the arising of new myths that will suffice to inspire us to go beyond the cocaine, the heroin, the depressions, and the suicides, through the inspiration of myths that lift us above a purely mundane existence."[21]

1
The Primordial Background

The mythological archetypes, which still guide us today, developed during the prehistoric time period, in the minds of our ancestors, when human tribes formed small hunter/gatherer societies as a means of survival.[22] In these early societies, the sexes were equal, each contributing to the good of the whole society.[23] The men hunted, and the women gathered herbs and wild grains and vegetables. As the human societies grew, game became scarce, and the society was forced into one of two alternatives. In some, people began to cultivate the grain and vegetables on their own.[24] In these early planting societies, survival depended on a "high accumulation of resources," and children of both sexes were taught to be responsible, to comply, and to put the needs of the group before those of the individual. Other groups continued to hunt, but in order to find enough game to sustain them, had to become transient societies, which could follow the giant herds of animals. In these groups, mobility was necessary for survival, and accumulations slowed the group down. Consumption was imperative. All children were taught to be aggressive and independent, and to be willing to take the risks that they would need for survival and successful hunting.[25]

In time, the planters came to think of God as a woman, Mother Earth, who gave birth to the plants and grains that formed the staple of their diets. It was the women who had learned the arts of cultivation, and who ran the farms.[26] To the women were accounted the "good" qualities of caring, compassion, and community. On the other hand, women in the hunting societies, which had to move frequently, were considered a burden, as it was difficult to move quickly with women and children, and the paraphernalia they had to bring with them. The men began to conceive of a male, hunting God, and attributed the "positive" values of independence and aggressive, risk-taking behavior to men.[27] Eventually, the hunters would learn to control the herds and it became necessary for them to protect large areas of land. Tribes of herders first began pillaging the settled villages and towns, eventually overtaking them and imposing their religion and values.

Since the farming societies had disdained aggression, they were in no shape to fight back. The cities that developed from these conquered villages developed a fear of "womanly" virtues, which might lead to weakness and defeat from other herding tribes, which were looking, of necessity, for places to conquer and settle. They imposed their gods and emphasized "masculine" traits.[28] From that time until now, women and the traits ascribed to them, traits of compliance, responsibility, compassion, have been devalued. It may be argued that this devaluation was necessary for the species to continue, since aggression from outsiders was a real threat, but several problems developed. For one thing, in these male-dominated cities, survival depended not only on defense, but also on that same "high accumulation" of goods that the earlier villages had. The problem was resolved through a division of labor. Two separate elements developed within the males of the society, with merchants and craftsmen constituting one group and warriors the other. The farmers, who had once been the primary force in the society, were moved to its outskirts. Modern society, like the earliest cities, is based primarily on the old planting way of life, with its overlay of herding traditions.

2
The Hero as Warrior

"The world-period of the hero in human form begins only when villages and cities have expanded over the land," writes Joseph Campbell in *Hero with a Thousand Faces.* He tells of "monsters" who "set themselves against the human community, [which] have to be cleared away," and of "tyrants of human breed, usurping to themselves the goods of their neighbors." "These have to be suppressed," he continues, and so, "The elementary deeds of the hero are those of the clearing of the field."[29]

It was at this time, as those first cities were developing, that the archetype of the hunter evolved into that of the warrior. For the earlier tribes, the gods and goddesses, who had ruled and granted favors or punishment as men deserved, were close at hand, but as those gods retreated, the concept of a human being capable of interceding between the society and its enemies came into being.[30] Carol Pearson defines a warrior as one who has accepted the necessity of taking human life in order to survive.[31] The warrior was honored as the defender of the territory. He protected the citizens from the invasion of greedy ogre-tyrants whose will to power caused them to take more land than they needed. So long as society depended on a land-based economy, war was inevitable, and the warrior, the primary hero.

3
The Childhood of the Mythological Hero

In *The Hero with a Thousand Faces*, Joseph Campbell explains that the mythical hero's childhood is a reconstruction developed many years after the hero's death, designed to prove that the future hero was predestined to achieve fame. This reconstructed pattern is always the same. From early infancy, the child goes through a period of deprivation and danger. He is often, from an early age, left to his own devices, where he finds "a zone of unsuspected presences, benign as well as malignant: an angel appears, a helpful animal, a fisherman, a hunter, crone or peasant." The hero is "fostered in the animal school, or... below ground... or, again, alone in some little room..." His primary teachers are the natural world, where, like the American Transcendentalists of the 1830's, he grasps the order and structure of the universe. He develops an almost mystical rapport with nature, with animals, and with the land itself. In his solitude, turning his attention inward, he learns to think things through for himself, and draws conclusions about the world based on his own internal perceptions of reality. Living an existence that would break many children, he survives, and develops both an extraordinary physical prowess and an uncanny strength of character that will develop his leadership potential. For a child growing up in these circumstances, Campbell tells us, "...an extraordinary capacity is required," even to survive[32]

Guches elaborates on those dangers and deprivations, pointing out that the hero loses, or is abandoned by, one or both of his natural parents, and is subsequently raised by foster parents and protective guardians.[33] Both of these sources correlate with Pearson's view of childhood as beginning in "Innocence," and leading to the child becoming an "Orphan."[34] During this period of "obscurity... extreme danger, impediment, or disgrace," Campbell tells us, when the "child of destiny" is, "thrown inward to his own depths or outward to the unknown, ... what he touches is a darkness unexplored"[35]

These mythical experiences, as noted earlier in this chapter, are usually reconstructed, psychically conceived in the mind of the hero's storytellers, long after his death.

Several individuals have noted the connection between myth and psychology. Marie Louise von Franz refers to Adolf Bastian's early studies on comparative mythology,[36] Rollo May to later works by Joseph Campbell.[37] Both von Franz and May develop the relationship between myth and the psychological processes first noted by Carl Jung, who introduced the concept of archetypes as they are encountered in our myths and dreams.[38] Marie-Louise von Franz explains that, "myth and mythical religious systems...are the first and foremost expression of objective psychic processes."[39] May calls myths, "our self-interpretation of our inner selves in relation to the outside world,"[40] and archetypes, "the structure of human existence."[41]

When one encounters a real human being, a man known for his personal heroism, whose actual childhood experiences are recent enough to be documented, and which fit that preconceived pattern, the reality of the myth and its archetypes, and their influence on our individual lives, becomes validated in human experience. Audie Murphy was such a man.

4
The Childhood of Audie Murphy

"I must have done some of my best fighting in a war I was in long before I joined the Army. You might say there never was a 'peace time' in my life, a time when things were good.... It was a full time job just existing."
       Audie Murphy
       "You Do the Prayin' and I'll Do the Shootin'"

At the time of Audie Murphy's birth, June 20, 1924 or '25, his mother, Josie Bell, had lost three of her six children. The youngest living child, June, was seven or eight. Corinne, the oldest, was fourteen or fifteen. He was born, then, in a rare space in his mother's life. She had time to care for him. Evidence indicates that, in spite of extreme poverty (they lived in a four-room shack), Audie's earliest years were relatively happy ones, even though when he was two, and his brother Richard was born (followed quickly by five other children in close succession), he was turned over to his sister Corinne. The arrangement seems to have been an agreeable one for both Corinne and Audie. Corinne seems to have been an exceptionally good caretaker. In fact, she seems to have taken this role for the entire family, but especially for Audie. She remembers him as having been a "happy child," who "laughed a great deal," whose "eyes just sparkled," even though his father, a farmhand, was unable to provide the family with even basic necessities.[42] Audie would say later, "Our situation [was] not to be blamed on the social structure. If my father had exercised more foresight, undoubtedly his family would have fared much better. He was not lazy, but he had a genius for not considering the future."[43] Audie's main source of support during these years was Corinne, who "rocked him to sleep many nights, singing to him...," kept him clean and neat, kept his hair cut, and gave in to his demands for cream gravy with his breakfast biscuits.[44]

But when Audie was five years old, Corinne married, and from that time on, he was left to his own devices. "From the time he could walk," according to Sue Gossett, author of *The Films and Career of Audie Murphy*, "his world was one of hard work -- by carrying wood to the house, and, at an early age, shooting game for the dinner table."[45] At five, he was reported by neighbors as being seen in the fields, "chopping corn and cotton, carrying firewood, [and] pulling onions."[46] When he got home at night, he had another chore: "massaging the tired, cramped fingers of his mother."[47] Audie's feelings about this part of his life are evident in the comments he would make later on. In 1953 he told a reporter, "Whenever my old man couldn't feed the kids he had, he got him another one."[48]

The family moved from one farm to another during the next few years. In his autobiography, *To Hell and Back*, Audie described his mother as being "a sad-eyed, silent woman who toiled eternally," and said, "She rarely talked. And she always seemed to be searching for something. What it was I don't know. We didn't discuss our feelings." As an adult he recalled, "the first thing I can remember was wanting to do something for her. I still feel guilty that I never could."[49]

When Audie was eight or nine, the family moved to Celeste, where his father went to work, briefly, for the WPA, and where, "for a time they lived in a converted boxcar on the edge of town," until they were able to afford to rent a "rundown house."[50]. That job would be no more successful than any of Emmett Murphy's previous endeavors. Still, Audie's situation did improve somewhat. He was able to go to school, where he performed quite well, in spite of frequent absences. His second grade teacher reported that "He was anxious to learn, and learned quickly. He loved to read and took great pride in his success at School... He seemed to love school and stayed late everyday... to see if there was something he could do to help me."[51]

It was also at this time that Audie bonded closely with two Celeste neighbors, "Mom" and "Barber" Cawthorn (Mr. Cawthorn was the town's barber.). "Mom" became a loving and attentive mother figure for him, and "Barber" taught him to hunt. Edward F. Murphy reports that he was a "natural marksman."[52] As the family's financial situation grew more desperate, Audie's .22 would often provide the only food the family had.[53]

Like Campbell's mythological children, Audie's helpers were not all human. When he was three, he acquired his first dog, "Wheeler."[54] Wheeler often protected Audie, even from his sister Corinne. The dog would not let her spank her little brother. Audie loved animals, especially dogs, and seemed to have an innate rapport with them.

Audie's physical and mental development during those years were exceptional. He was clearly a gifted child, physically as well as mentally. Although he was small for his age he was "well-coordinated" and his "eyesight and his bearing were almost perfect. For his size he had large strong hands and very long fingers, allowing him to handle a gun with ease."[55] " He displayed an uncanny accuracy with a rifle," and "possessed catlike reflexes, quick eyes, and an aggressive personality."[56]

Again, like the children in the myths, Audie spent much of his time by himself. He developed a habit of going off alone, frightening the family. "He was constantly getting lost. Once he ran away for the day and found the neighborhood folks searching the swimming hole when he strolled back `a la Tom Sawyer"[57] In later years he would remember that he, "was never so happy as when alone. In my solitude," he said, "my dreams made sense."[58]

His social development did indicate some problems. The same second grade teacher reported, "He seemed to carry a chip on his shoulder. I always thought of him as my Fighting Irishman."[59] In *To Hell and Back*, Audie explained why: "...I had just one pair of overalls. My mother washed them every night by the kitchen stove. They shrunk halfway to my knees. So the guys started calling me short-britches, and I'd slug them. I fought every day."[60] In later years, he would write, "God knows where my pride came from, but I had it. And it was constantly getting me into trouble. My temper was explosive. And my moods, typically Irish, swung from the heights to the depths. At school, I fought a great deal. Perhaps I was trying to level with my fists what I assumed fate had put above me."[61]

But Audie's anger, and his willingness to fight back, were indications of some positive factors he brought from his early childhood. He had access to his aggression, and a highly developed sense of injustice. He recognized that he was being treated unfairly and he took action to stop it. Defending himself apparently worked; he made several life-long friends during those school years.[62]

His success in academics, his physical coordination, his willingness to take on adult responsibilities, his hunting skills, the closeness with the Cawthorn's, all helped to overcome the obvious problems. But this is the natural time for a boy to enter the world of his father and leave the mother. Audie was unable to leave his mother because he had to become his own father, and act as both parents for his brothers and sisters. His youngest sister, Nadene, spoke to reporter Brad Kellar of the *Greenville Herald Banner* during May of 1997. "In the wintertime," she told Kellar, "we'd be freezing and there'd be three, four, five us in the bed. Audie would make up stories to tell to get our minds off our hungry stomachs." Kellar reports she recalled many nights that "they would be lulled to sleep by the sound of their older brother's voice."[63]

When he was twelve or thirteen, he had to quit school to work full time, and left home to make things easier on his younger brothers and sisters.[64] He lived for a time with a farmer named Haney Lee, whom he always referred to as "General," and his wife. While he was living there, Haney Lee taught him to drive a car. The Lee's say that in 1937, he "did a man's work," that he was "very neat and polite and a fanatic about cleanliness." Mrs. Lee described him as being, "very timid and withdrawn ...very proud." Another acquaintance from this period, Goldie Warren, says he was, "...oh, so honest, humble, shy, proud, and neat as a pin.... He was a good worker, and tried, on what little he had, to help his family..."[65] Even at this early age, he had already become a very different boy from the baby who always laughed.

As he entered adolescence, things got worse instead of better. After quitting school and moving out of the house, he still gave his mother what little money he had, and continued to hunt for food. He had several close male friends, but girls, at that time, were a different matter. "When I was fourteen and felt moony about a girl, I did all of my admiring from a long distance off," he wrote years later. "I was too ashamed to come closer. There were my short britches. There were my home repaired shoes--the soles stitched to the uppers with bailing wire. And there was the time that would be wasted if I talked to her that I might better spend picking up wood for my mother, or chopping for hire."[66]

About that time, his father, who had been disappearing for longer and longer periods of time, left permanently. Audie said, "I suppose I hated him because I hate anyone who quits."[67] Before long, he was taking over the roles of both breadwinner and caretaker for the family. His mother, an old woman at forty-nine, retired to her bed and died a few months later. He explained, "In a home where food was hard to come by, medicine and treatment were unattainable luxuries, not necessities... Her story, including her early death, is not unusual in a sharecropper's family, particularly when the sharecropper himself runs off, leaving his wife to take care of their children--in Mother's case, nine of us."[68]

"My older sisters had married and left home," he wrote in 1956, "leaving me as the oldest.... I was fully aware that I had a wage-earners role as the oldest male in the house. And, of course, I couldn't make enough money, picking up odd jobs that a boy can do, to help much.... and back of it all was the shadow of my father, for whom my hate grew stronger and stronger as the burdens he had thrown off piled up on me."[69]

Audie Murphy understood one thing about himself quite clearly. He could hunt. Hunting had provided him the means of survival. His feelings against his father were too strong for him to choose options. He only knew he didn't want to be anything like him. Although he never actually rebelled against his mother, he could not accept her blind faith in a loving God. He learned his religious concepts the same way that other, earlier hunters had done. His religion was the way of the "shaman." Left to his own devices, he studied nature, where Campbell says the mythological child finds "a zone of unsuspected presences, benign as well as malignant: an angel appears, a helpful animal, a fisherman, a hunter, crone or peasant." The hero is "fostered in the animal school, or... below ground... or, again, alone in some little room..."[70] Like these future heroes of myth, Audie Murphy was, "thrown outward, into the world of nature, [where] he developed a lasting rapport with animals; [and] inward, to his own thoughts," and in that "darkness unexplored" spoken of by Campbell, somehow found the strength, not only to survive, but to become extraordinary.

    Not long after Audie's mother died, his younger brother and sisters were placed in an orphanage.[71] Throughout his life, Audie would carry a profound sense of responsibility toward others, which began during these childhood years, and a deeply felt guilt for not having been able to support his family.

    A few months later, fate intervened. Japan bombed Pearl Harbor.

BOOK I: THE HERO'S JOURNEY

PART I: SEPARATION

1
The Call to Adventure

The bombing of Pearl Harbor signaled the beginning of Audie Murphy's "Call to Adventure," which Joseph Campbell calls, "…first stage of the mythological journey." The call, "signifies that destiny has summoned the hero and transferred his spiritual center of gravity from within the pale of his society to a zone unknown." At this time the hero is summoned to leave his "everyday hut or castle," and begin his journey into a, "fateful region of both treasure and danger." The place of adventure can take several different forms: "a distant land, a forest, a kingdom underground, beneath the waves, or above the sky, a secret island, lofty mountaintop, or prolonged dream state." It is always," Campbell continues, "a place of strangely fluid and polymorphous beings, unimaginable torments, superhuman deeds, and impossible delights."[72]

Some potential heroes refuse the call, at least for a while, usually because the parents hold him back. "One is bound in by the walls of childhood; the father and mother stand as threshold guardians, and the timorous soul, fearful of some punishment, fails to make the passage through the door and come to birth in the world without..."[73] But when Audie's mother died, he was sixteen years old. His father had left the family. His brothers and sisters had been taken from his care. He had nowhere to go, and "Hell," he later wrote, "could not be any worse than the particular part of Texas that I came from."[74]

So Audie Leon Murphy, set out on his first journey, answering the "call to adventure." Every individual who chooses to answer the call relies on his inner knowledge of the archetypal Hero, the courageous youth who "goes into battle" to slay the "ogre-tyrant." The motherless boy went off to war--envisioning a "faraway battlefield, where bugles blew, banners streamed, and men charged gallantly across flaming hills; where the temperature always stood at eighty and our side was always victorious; where the wounded never cried; where enemy bullets always missed me and my trusty rifle forever hit home."[75]

For a young man who leaves home to literally go off to war, the symbolic journey becomes terribly real, and the archetypal figures take on an even greater significance, especially if the child has been underprotected. If the real parents have been negative forces, the dangers of the journey are harder to overcome. The hazards to the young hero's soul, or psyche, are increasingly perilous.

2
Supernatural Aid

"The first encounter of the hero-journey," according to Campbell, "is with a protective figure (often a little old crone or old man) who provides the adventurer with amulets against the dragon forces he is about to pass."[76] And so our potential hero, Audie Murphy, left home when he was barely 17, armed with "amulets" given him by his "helpers," various friends and neighbors from Celeste and the surrounding area. During World War II, nearly half of the 400-plus men who won the Congressional Medal of Honor died in battle. Of the men who returned, nearly half brought back emotional and physical problems that would prevent them from living successfully. Those remaining who were successful were relatively older when they went to war, and better educated, having completed high school, and attended college. They came from families that were relatively functional. The "amulets" of education and stable homes helped these men through that "dark journey of the soul."

Audie's amulets were somewhat meager. He had his hunting skills, which he had developed with the help of John Cawthorn, and the meals provided by the Springfields, a farming family Audie worked for during the last months before his enlistment. (Beatrice Springfield, the family's daughter, said later that he even, "filled up on vegetables he didn't like," to make sure he reached the proper weight. Audie, at the time, stood about 5' 5" and weighed about 115 pounds.)[77] In addition, he had a letter from his sister Corinne to back up a birth certificate, which declared him to be eighteen years old. Both documents were probably inaccurate. Phillip T. Washburn of the *Fort Hood Sentinel* wrote that his birth certificate "was filed only 90 days before he enlisted," and that "there may have never been an original birth certificate. That would not have been unusual for the time and place Murphy was born.... On a passport application filed in the late 1960s, he listed his birth date as 1925, which would have made him 17 and underage when he headed for basic training."[78] Apparently Corinne recognized his need to begin his journey, and lied for him.

In the Arthur Penn movie, "Little Big Man," a "wise old man" named Old Lodge Skins gives the young Jack Crabb a new name. In Native American cultures, one of the amulets a young warrior receives is an adult name, which he earns, as opposed to the names given him as a child. Crabb was given the name Little Big Man, because, according to Old Lodge Skins, "his body was little, but his heart was big."[79] When he left home, Audie Leon Murphy had but the two names given him by his parents. He had also been given other names, none of which he was proud; he was sometimes called "Little Pat," after his father,[80] and there was the derisive name "Short Britches," given by his schoolmates. To his mother he was Audie, the "little man," who looked after her when her husband would not. He preferred to be called by his middle name, Leon.[81] The power of these names is evident in the Audie, who always carried so much responsibility, and the fighting "lion," Leon, who was willing to do battle with anyone who called him "Short Britches." But he would soon earn an adult name. After being stuck with "Baby" during his early training, his buddies would give him a more respectful title: "Murph"[82]

3
Crossing the First Threshold

Audie Leon Murphy is now ready to respond to his Call to Adventure, which Campbell tells us, "rings up the curtain, always, on a mystery of transfiguration--a rite, or moment, of spiritual passage, which, when complete, amounts to a dying and a birth. The familiar life horizon has been outgrown; the old concepts, ideals, and emotional patterns no longer fit; the time for the passing of a threshold is at hand."[83] But crossing that threshold into the land of adventures and darkness is not that easy. First the hero has to conquer the "Threshold Guardians," whose job it is to see that no unworthy candidate begins the journey, "for beyond... there is darkness, the unknown, and danger."[84]

Here, Audie had to contend with his obvious youth and size. "...I hurried to the Marine Corps recruiting station," he wrote in *To Hell and Back*. "This branch seemed the toughest of the lot; and I was looking for trouble. Unfortunately, the corps was looking for men, men italicized. A sergeant looked over my skinny physique. My weight did not measure up to Leatherneck standards.... My pride was taking an awful beating. The sergeant was the first in a long line of uniformed authorities that I requested to go to the devil."[85] But Audie Murphy would not be held back. After being turned down by the paratroops as well, was finally accepted by the Infantry. Still, the "guardians" were at work. His first days as a recruit did not help. "During my first session of close order drill, I, the late candidate for the marines and the paratroops, passed out cold. I quickly picked up the nickname 'Baby,'"[86] He later told Thomas B. Morgan that, "He had a series of bloody noses because he was too light to control the Army's standard bolt action .03 rifle. 'It kept kicking me in the face,'" he told Morgan, "'and I barely qualified with it.'" According to Morgan, "he sagged dangerously under his regulation sixty-pound sack, until he learned to stuff it with toilet paper instead of the usual gear."[87] As a result of these instances, as he said in *To Hell and Back*, "[his] commanding officer tried to shove [him] into a cook and baker's school…"[88] Later, other well-meaning officers would try to make him a stateside clerk. But he soon taught them. In spite of his small size and poor beginning, he excelled in his training, and showed not only great fighting skill, but the ability to get along with others: "Murph had a knack of talking to officers. He was neat in dress, courteous, and had a good training record, so they listened to him," said fellow enlistee Walter "Blackie" Black, according to Harold Simpson in *Audie Murphy: American Soldier*.[89]

Eventually, he and his "companions of the hunt" were ready to proceed into what Campbell calls "The Belly of the Whale," after the biblical story of Jonah and several other mythological adventures.[90] They spent eleven days in the belly of a troop ship called the *Hawaiian Shipper*, many of them, including Audie, seasick most of the time. The ship took him to North Africa, where he would undergo further training designed to hone his warrioring skills and prepare him mentally for the dangers of war.[91]

4
The Belly of the Whale

Private Audie Leon Murphy began his "night sea journey" on February 6, 1943, aboard the troop ship that took him to North Africa, where he would join "Baker" Company, 1st Battalion, 15th Infantry Regiment, Third Division, which specialized in amphibious landings. The division's leader was the now-famous General Lucian Truscott. Audie was "not overjoyed" with the Infantry at first. It "was too commonplace for my ambition." He wrote in *To Hell and Back*, "[But] the months would teach me the spirit of this unglamorous, greathearted fighting machine." He would soon realize that, "In Africa they knew what to train for. I learned to hike five miles an hour--almost a trot until you got used to it.... I learned to go 24 hours on a canteen of water and the weather was really hot. That's the kind of training that gets a guy ready for really tough battlefield work."[92] The "trot" he referred to was the "Truscott Trot" which involved "…a marching speed of 5 mph. for one hour, 4 mph. For the next two hours, and 3 1/2 mph. for the rest of the thirty-mile march."[93] On March 15, Simpson writes that Murph moved with his division to the "Army Invasion Training Center at Arzew, a Mediterranean port just north of Oram, Algeria. Here, the 3rd Division engaged in intensive combat, amphibious, and combined operations training." The plans for an Allied Invasion of Sicily were underway. Of the division's nine battalions, "four were trained in direct beach assault, and four, including the 1st Battalion, 15th Infantry, to which Audie was assigned, were trained to pass through the assault battalions and seize inland objectives. The remaining battalion was specially trained in street fighting."[94] On May 7, Murph would receive his first promotion, to PFC. From this time until a week or so after the landing at Licata Beach in Sicily, he would serve as runner for his platoon. On June 22, the division participated in a practice called "Operation Copybook... a dry run so realistic that it appeared to some of the participants to be the real thing."[95] At this time several "senior officers expressed the opinion that, 'never, anywhere, was a combat division more fit for combat...more in readiness to close with the enemy than the 3rd Infantry Division.'"

Finally, on July 4, as the Division was getting ready to leave (on another sea-journey), a Review and Awards Ceremony was held, and Truscott spoke directly to the men. "The sun was hot. His spirited speech was short. He ended it with, 'You are going to meet the Boche. Carve your name on his face!'"[96] Leon, the hunter was becoming "Murph," the warrior. His North Africa training complete, he returned to the "whale's belly" for another "night sea journey." This time the "whale," an LCT, would literally spit him ashore on the beaches of Sicily.

PART 2: INITIATION
(The Dark Side of the journey)

The Road of Trials

Having crossed the threshold successfully, the hero begins his journey down the "Road of Trials," which Campbell refers to as "the favorite phase of the mythic journey." He is about to endure a series of tests, each more difficult than the last, where he must meet and conquer the forces of darkness if he is to survive. Each test or trial has a lesson the hero must learn in order to take the next step along the road. More and more horrifying events unfold, as he approaches the "nadir of the journey, the "darkest part of the forest," where he battles the dragon, and that battle becomes not only a struggle for life, but for his soul as well[97]

1
Sicily
The Lesson of Reality

The LCT carrying Murph and his companions chugged through the night toward the shores of Sicily and their first encounter with the dark forces along the "Road of Trials."[98] Their thoughts would have been much the same as Samuel E. Morison described in his multi-volume study of World War Two's naval operations. "There is nothing in warfare, or perhaps even in life, to be compared with the hushed mystery of the final approach in a night landing. Everything ahead is uncertain. There is no sound but the rush of waters, the throbbing of your ship's engines and of your heart.... There can be no drawn battle, no half-success, in an amphibious landing; it is win all splendidly or lose all miserably."[99] So Murph rode through the night, frightened, and likely seasick, toward a destiny which had been decided from the time he first landed in North Africa.

Projecting a successful outcome of the North African campaign, the Allied forces had been planning the early stages of an advance into Europe. The Allies next objective in the Mediterranean would be Sicily. "At the Casablanca Conference in January 1943, the Americans and the British had agreed they were not ready to invade Europe across the English Channel. Sicily, with its airfields, was a logical choice."[100] The decision was made, "with four major objects in view: (1) securing the Mediterranean line of communications, (2) diverting German forces from the Russian front, (3) increasing the pressure on Italy, and

(4) creating 'a situation in which Turkey [could] be enlisted as an active ally.'"[101]

One day later a "rough plan" for what was now being called Operation HUSKY was underway, described by B. H. Liddell Hart as, "a converging sea approach and invasion by forces coming from the eastern and western Mediterranean respectively."[102] General Eisenhower would lead the forces. British General Alexander would be his second-in-command. Exactly what form the actual operation would take was argued by the generals and admirals for several months while the GI's, including Audie Murphy, trained in North Africa. The final plan for Operation HUSKY was finally approved on May 13, six days after Murphy's promotion to PFC., and the same day as the collapse of the Axis forces in Tunisia. The plan had Admiral Hewitt's Western Task Force landing on the "south coast between Licata and Scoglitti, while the British Eastern Task Force concentrated on the Pachino Peninsula and the Gulf of Noto, short of Syracuse," according to Morison.[103] Harold Simpson pointed out that, "The narrow strait between Italy and Sicily, the Allies knew, would be well fortified, so a strategic decision was made to land on the southeastern shores of the island."[104]

It was a bold plan. "HUSKY," wrote Edward F. Murphy in *The Heroes of WWII*, "would be the largest amphibious operation in history."[105]   According to B. H. Liddle Hart, "...the assault landing, by eight divisions simultaneously, was larger in scale even than in Normandy eight months later.... the ultimate total [number of troops] was about 478,000---250 British, 228,000 American"[106] The landing would not be without its particular problems. "The Sicilian beaches and shores were far from ideal for amphibious landings...the gradients were too easy, and the beaches were fronted by 'false beaches.'" One of the major problems for such a large undertaking would involve getting vast numbers of reinforcements and supplies safely ashore, because, as he points out, "the era when the Navy could land soldiers and sail away was long past. A modern army, even if it meets little opposition, must be continually fed provisions, motor fuel, clothing, and all manner of materiel.... A shuttle of LST's and Liberty ships was provided to run the stuff into Sicily quickly."[107]   Once landed, "...the American and British armies were to proceed via the shallow coastal shelves on either side of Mt. Etna to Messina."[108]

General Patton's Seventh Army, which was landed by Hewitt's task force, consisted of three attack forces: JOSS, the Licata force, Truscott's 3rd Infantry Division and two Ranger battalions, DIME, the Gela force, and CENT, the Scoglitti force. Morison reported that, "The 3rd Division, which had fought in Operation TORCH, was given the honor of handling the important left flank of the Sicilian assault."[109] Simpson added that "Patton's initial objective, after capturing the coastal towns and close-in airports...was to drive north across the island to cut off Axis reinforcements moving east."[110]

Morison described the scene in front of the landing forces in detail. "The shore extends 37 miles from the Torre di Gaffe to Porto Braccato, and on its rim are two small cities, Licata and Gela, and a fishing village, Scoglitti, convenient foci for the three American attack groups--JOSS, DIME, and CENT. Over half the shoreline is sand beach; the rest, rocky points and low cliffs.... Three rivers, the Salso, the Gela, and the Acate, empty into the gulf, flowing through flat and coastal plains." The 3rd Division's JOSS force was split into four attack groups: Gafi, Molla, Salso (the 1st and 3rd Battalions of the 15th Regiment, which would land at Beach Yellow), and Falconara.[111]

On June 23, 1943, General Eisenhower's Naval aide, Captain Henry C. "Harry" Butcher made this entry in his journal: "More than 1000 ocean-going vessels – transport and escort – will be in HUSKY...The thousand figure does not include small landing craft, small escort vessels and coasters. We will have 149,000 men in the first wave – 10,000 more than landed in Casablanca, Oran, and Algiers attacks. We will attack on an eighty-mile front."[112]

PFC. Murphy was about to learn that 20th Century warfare, with its mass technology, was a far cry from war as he had imagined it to be back home. And yet, for the foot soldier, in hand-to-hand combat, the influence of the early hunting tribes was still evident. General Truscott, "had intensively trained his division in the right sort of tactics to meet the situation. The first battalion ashore was to 'work like a pack of hounds, hunting out beach defenses and keeping them occupied while the remaining infantry battalions, by-passing resistance, penetrate inland to consolidate key areas.'" The tactics are the same as those used by the early hunters about to surround the animals they were attacking. Murph and his fellow GI's were ready for a rapid advance, having been "landed in light order, carrying only their own weapons, two canteens of water per man, gas mask, and combat pack for toilet kit, K-rations, and extra ammunition...." The rest of their gear remained aboard ship, to be deployed after the beachhead was secure.[113]

On July 10, D-day for the Sicily landings, Ike's aide, Captain Butcher wrote again in his journal: "...the Royal Navy Signal Officer...phoned me to say he had a signal from Admiral Hewitt...the Gela landings... had been made at 2:45 on schedule, followed by succeeding waves of landings. No enemy action of surface ships. No enemy air action. No mines. Slight opposition from shore....They have taken Gela, Hewitt indicated. Good work...but no news yet as to [the other two American units]...the 3rd under Truscott, is shooting for Licata, perhaps the toughest of all."[114]

"About 3000 yards east of the Salso River, separated from it by a marshy tract and a pond, begins Beach Yellow;"[115] wrote Morison. The city of Licata lay just to the left, with Monte Solo behind it. Directly ahead lay Saffarello Hill and Monte Gallardo. The landing went well, as Simpson reported: "The 1st Battalion came ashore at Beach Yellow just east of the town of Licata. Enemy opposition was light."[116] Although Harold Simpson wrote that PFC. Murphy was a part of those first landings and "apparently got ashore without incident,"[117] it is likely that he did not. "Just leave it to the Army to foul things up," Murph wrote in *To Hell and Back*, "If the schedule had not gone snafu, we would have come ashore with the assault forces. That was what I wanted. I had primed myself for the big moment. Then the timing got snarled in the predawn confusion, and we came in late, chugging ashore like a bunch of clucks in a ferryboat."[118] Murph's own account is backed up by Morison who reported that the Salso landings went extremely well except for "nine LCT's destined for Beach Yellow [which] lost sight of their guide and ran blind." They followed the wrong guide boat, and headed for the Gela River with DIME force. "But the mistake was remedied after daylight and those LCT's reached Beach Yellow at 0800,"[119] completely in accord with Murph's recollections.

It appears that Murph didn't miss more than a little sporadic resistance. "Within ninety minutes of landing, some units had moved over one mile inland." The "successive assault waves," Murph and his group included, "raced shoreward, adding depth to the initial punch," encountering only "occasional counterattacks by German and Italian armor... By nightfall, the Allied beachheads were very much intact."[120]

On July 13, Captain Butcher accompanied Ike on a visit to Sicily, where they observed from Admiral Hewitt's command ship, the *Monrovia*. "...we found General Patton in good spirits.... he showed us [on a map] that the American invasion was well up to, if not ahead of, the schedule in all sectors....General Truscott, with his promising 3rd Division, had lived up to expectations."[121]

Truscott's "Trotters," PFC Murphy included, moved quickly through their initial objectives, "thrusting," as Morison continued, both "north and west." The Italians were reinforced, and tried, "to create a semicircle from Cancatti to a point southwest of Agrigento...but the 3rd Division never gave them a chance to get together." The 3rd had captured Cancatti by the 12th of July.[122]

The 3rd Division's next step was to advance on Agrigento. During that march, PFC Murphy was frustrated over having been made a runner for his platoon, since his commander, seeing his obvious youth and small size, wanted to protect him. But Murph, at this point still eager to be a part of the fighting, would slip off and join patrols until the commander realized his abilities, and on July 15, promoted him to corporal, and put him in charge of a squad.[123] From that point, he was heavily involved in the fighting as, "over the twisted, potholed mountain roads the GIs overcame numerous strong points, and entered [Agrigento] from the east. Sporadic fighting broke out, but by 3:00 a. m. on July 17, Agrigento was in American hands."[124]

The American commanders were determined that their forces would put in a better showing in this campaign than the British. "'I want you to be in Palermo in five days' was the word received by the 3rd division from General Truscott on 18 July after taking a brief rest after the capture of Agrigento. The city was a hundred miles distant, by two roughly parallel roads over country almost devoid of water and studded by several strong points. Yet they did it on foot in four days."[125]

Leaving the Agrigento area on the 19th of July, Corporal Murphy and the rest of the 3rd began to advance on Palermo, on roads "which [wound] up to 2500-foot elevations, with barely 400 yards of level going at a time, encounter[ing] demolitions in the shape of blown bridges, tunnels, and tank traps. Wheat stubble and harvested bean fields bordered the roads, and springs of sweet water were few and far between." The heat was intense, and Morison described the thick dust as "A compound of cattle dung and pulverized chalky rock."[126]

In *To Hell and Back*, corporal Murphy wrote that the march, "became virtually a foot-race," Averaging "from twenty-five to thirty miles a day over rugged terrain." He, too, spoke of the extremity of the physical conditions: "Dust lay over the highways like a smoke screen; not a cloud appeared in the sky. Often we could not stop to eat. We gulped our rations as we walked."[127]

Morison reports that the competition between the Americans and British was hardly less fierce than that among the American leaders themselves. "According to General Truscott General Patton ordered the 3rd Division to hold back so he could make a triumphal entry with the 2nd Armored. This plan was somewhat spoiled by a delegation of the municipality insisting on surrounding the city by the infantry, so that it could obtain troops to keep order. The GI's got there first."[128]

Later, in 1953, Murphy would recall that competitiveness with a touch of bitterness. "I remember a thirty-five mile forced march up and down mountains that ended us up with bleeding feet just because our brass wanted to beat Patton to Palermo," he told reporter Richard Hubler of the *Saturday Evening Post*.[129] That bitterness may be explained by Murph's account of his reaction to the heat and dust. A day or so before the division reached Palermo, the young corporal grew ill. Too dizzy to continue marching, he fell out and, "heaved until I thought I would lose my stomach."[130] When a major riding in a relatively comfortable jeep drove by and asked if he was ill, which was rather obvious, the young corporal replied, a bit sarcastically, "Nosir. I'm just spilling my guts for the hell of it." The major suggested he might report to the medics, but Murph was determined to see the march through. "I rose to my feet and staggered up the road, cursing the war in detail."[131] But the heat and dust had caught up with Murph. The next day he collapsed, and spent a week in the hospital while his buddies enjoyed a week's leave in Palermo. He recovered just in time to leave for San Stefano by train with the rest of his division as the 7th Army proceeded along the upper coast of Sicily toward Messina.[132] "By midnight, August 1, the entire 3rd Division was concentrated on the

Tornamuzza Plain west of San Stefano, on the edge of the Tyrolean Sea."[133]

The German/Italian resistance was stronger along the coast than it had been on the march northward, It took the 3rd a week to move from San Stefano to San Fratello. The heat was still intense, and water was scarce. The Germans retreated slowly, leaving mines and rear-guard emplacements on various ridges along the way. By the time they finally reached San Fratello, "the German reserves had time to construct field fortifications, which they and the Assieta Division held so well that the 3rd Division was held up for five days."[134]

"It is a tedious race for Messina," writes Captain Butcher on the 12th of August. "The roads and bridges are demolished by the slowly retreating enemy. Mines are everywhere. Truscott's 3rd Division has made successful amphibious landings behind the enemy's lines on the north coast, the first one resulting in 1500 prisoners, 300 or which were German. We haven't the details on the second yet, but were told it was successful."[135]

Corporal Murphy's account of the situation indicates that he is learning well the lesson of the reality of war. "The enemy is entrenched and determined.... On our approach to the stream, we are caught in a concentration of artillery and mortar fire. The earth is shuddering; and the screaming of shells intermingles with the screaming of men. We fall back, reorganize, and again storm forward. For a second time the barrage hits us. Again we withdraw." This time, when Murph is pulled from the front as part of a guard for a machine gun emplacement, he doesn't complain. "The assignment suits me. I now see that the fighting will not run out. There will be plenty of war for everybody." He has also learned to take advantage of any brief respites from the fighting. "While the battle grows in violence, I lie in a vineyard, eating grapes and watching the fight…. I contributed little to the battle; gained much. I acquired a healthy respect for the Germans as fighters; and insight into the fury of combat; and a bad case of diarrhea. I had eaten too many grapes."[136]

Relief is at hand. German General Fries began the evacuation of San Fratello the next day, because, as Morison reported, "The capture of Troina by the 1st Division had laid the Fratello position open to attack from the south and forced the General's decision." The rest of the push to Messina was relatively easy, as the Germans continued to evacuate, leaving the island open to the approaching Allies.[137]

"ALGIERS, TUESDAY, AUGUST 17, 1943," begins Butcher's journal entry, "Truscott's 3rd Division entered Messina at 8 o'clock last night. Yesterday at the meeting of the Commanders-in-Chief at La Marsa, one of the British officers – Brigadier Sugden – said he knew jolly well that Patton, after driving his

Seventh Army all over Sicily, would be the first into Messina and, he said, "He's got the Eighth Army bloody well surrounded." Sugden was right."[138]

Corporal Murphy's first trial is at an end. He has learned its lesson well. He wrote of it in *To Hell and Back*: "The Sicilian campaign has taken the vinegar out of my spirits. I have seen war as it actually is and I do not like it."[139] He cannot be aware, at this point, that this campaign is only the first in a progressively more harrowing set of trials along the dark road of adventure. As Edward F. Murphy wrote in *Heroes of World War II,* "For the Americans, the thirty-eight-day fight for Sicily provided a valuable preview of the fighting that lay ahead in Italy. The battle for the Italian peninsula would prove to be an eighteen month struggle."[140]

2
Salerno to the Mignano Gap
The Lesson of Irony

"Even before Sicily was invaded...events were taking place that would force the Allies to continue their drive in the Mediterranean," writes William L Allen.[141] The Allies at this time were in a difficult position. Eisenhower believed that the main thrust of the European Invasion should be a direct attack on France. But he was well aware that it was too early for its launching to be successful. Churchill, on the other hand, believed that the best place to concentrate their forces was on the Axis powers "soft underbelly," and was pushing for an attack on the Italian mainland.[142]

A decisive moment in the decision-making occurred when Mussolini was over thrown. At that point, "...the imminent Italian surrender, and the ease with which Sicily was captured, a decision by the allies to undertake a major campaign on the mainland became more of a certainty."[143]

All factors combined to lead to the invasion of Italy. The Allies were to keep as many of the German forces as possible engaged in its defense, to keep them away from the Russian Front until the invasion of France proved more feasible. The plans quickly got underway. "On 26 July, Lieutenant General

Mark Clark, commander of the newly formed U. S. Fifth Army... received a 'planning task' known as AVALANCHE. This one called for an amphibious assault in the vicinity of Naples, most likely the Bay of Salerno." The planning for AVALANCE continued throughout August. "General Clark selected the 36th Division, commanded by an old friend, Major General Fred Walker, for the main thrust at Salerno because it had 'good leadership and high caliber personnel'" In addition to the 36th, the 45th Division would make the initial attack. The 3rd and 46th Divisions would remain in Messina, to be called on if needed.[144]

Edward Murphy felt that the Germans were hoping for the choice to be Salerno. " German commander, Field Marshal Albert Kesselring, called the commanding heights [around Salerno] 'God's gift to the gunners.' And once the beachhead was consolidated, the Allies would have to move through Naples through the formidable Sorrento Hills, in which there were only two narrow, easily defended gorges."[145]

While Corporal Murphy and the rest of the 3rd Division rested and trained at Messina, "AVALANCHE became a reality when at 0330 a. m. on 9 September, elements of General Walker's 36th Division began their long, difficult trek up the Italian mainland by stepping on the shores of Salerno."[146]

General Clark had hoped for a surprise

attack, but as B. H. Liddell Hart reported in *The History of the Second World War*, "The approach of the convoys, made round the north and east coasts of Sicily, were spotted and reported to the German headquarters early in the afternoon of the 8th, and at 3:30 p. m., their troops were put on the alert in readiness for the expected landing." [147]

As a result, when the members of the 36th Division hit the beach, they were greeted with a loudspeaker message in English: "Come on in, You're covered."[148]

The 36th, joined the next day by the 45th, gave everything they had, but Kesselring was equally determined they would not succeed, and as Allen wrote, "...the German reaction began to take the form of a determined effort to drive the British and American invaders back into the Tyrrhenian Sea."[149]

Kesselring's counterattack was fierce, so much so that at the end of the first week, the 3rd Division was called in to reinforce the invasion troops. The additional troops turned the tide. After the 3rd entered the fray, Kesselring began a slow withdrawal into the Apennine Mountains. "...Part of [his] master plan was to make the Allies pay dearly for every foot of Italian soil,"[150]

On September 16, Harry Butcher wrote in his journal, "General Ike had been required to make a command decision that the landings at Salerno Bay would be made despite the planners' qualms over the shortage of landing craft and denial of our request for temporary use of additional bombers. He had the support of the land, sea, and air commanders...but the responsibility still remains his. Now, with Clark in trouble, Ike is moving heaven and earth to help him and his 5th Army...Landing craft intended to bring up service troops of assault division have been diverted to bring the 3rd Division, resting in Sicily, into the battle of Salerno."[151]

On September 21, Corporal Murphy and his regiment came ashore near Battipaglia, and quickly worked into the mountains near Curticelli. Harold Simpson wrote that, "For the next fifty days the 3rd Division never lost contact with the enemy for more than a few hours at a time."[152]

"Through the jagged ridges and valleys of the Apennines the GI's pursued the Germans north toward Naples. Combat in the mountains of Italy was worse than in Sicily. There was little flat land for deployment of armored vehicles," wrote Edward Murphy. "Italy would be an infantryman's war.'[153]

One week after the landing, on Sept 28, the 3rd captured the town of Avellino. "The movement from Curticelli to the vicinity of Avellino was made on foot," according to Simpson. "Supplies were transported by pack animals, and on occasion soldiers back-packed food and ammunition to the outposts of the mountains."[154]

On October 1, Naples fell to the British forces, but by the 3 of October, Murphy's 15th Regiment was "slowed down by enemy demolitions [and] had advanced but a few miles, to a position just south of Cancello. Here, on a ridge east of town the regiment was held up for a day by enemy self-propelled artillery and machine gun fire," according to Simpson.[155]

Corporal Murphy and his squad were right in the middle of the fight. These men had become a close-knit group. Having fought through Sicily together, they trusted each other and they trusted their squad leader. The camaraderie of the "hunting companions" dates back to the earliest hunting societies, when the bond of the hunters was vital to the outcome of the hunt. In these societies, small groups about the size of a modern platoon, leaders would emerge whenever a member of the group possessed a certain courage and audacity that would gain him the respect of his fellow hunters. These circumstances led to a natural selection of the leader who possessed the best skill. The same thing happens today, especially in the smaller military units. Leaders are promoted in the field when they show this audacity, and gain the respect of their immediate comrades. In wartime, platoon leaders develop from out of this natural skill, as Audie Murphy had been doing, not only from the early days in Sicily, but during stateside training as well. In the heat of battle, surfaces are dropped. Age, background, wealth, formal education and social acceptance hold little interest to the foot soldier, who chooses to follow based on his leader's natural ability. At this level, the "companions" have a strong voice in the choosing, even if it is not official. The junior officers who make such decisions know whom the men will follow.

Corporal Murphy's report of this march toward Cancello illustrates a prime example of that relationship. "The dash [to Rome] has slowed to a push....We sit in a ditch near a road northeast of Salerno. Ahead a bridge over a shallow stream has been blown; and just beyond the ruins is an enemy machine-gun emplacement."[156]

The men in Murphy's platoon seem content to sit back and take the opportunity to engage in light banter as they anticipate some "heavy scrapping ahead." But eighteen-year-old Corporal Murphy, already a seasoned leader, quickly points out that the gun "has to be knocked out." Amid more banter, Steiner and Brandon volunteer to move out with him.

After crawling through the woods, they reach the stream. "It is almost dry," he writes, "The banks are lined with brush. We can advance up the bed in a crouching walk." But Steiner reaches an open area and is dropped by a machine gun blast. The next move is up to

Brandon, but Murph reports that "Suddenly a picture pops into my mind. It is that of his nine-year old daughter... 'Deer daddy i am in school...'" and quickly thinks, "Let the war wait." Brandon is prone to take risks, and Murph doesn't want to see another child orphaned, but Brandon is already moving, tossing grenades as Murph fires his tommy gun. They take the emplacement, killing five Germans in the process. "Brandon surveys the scene with a frown on his face," Murphy recalls. "'Jesus,' he says. And from his manner of speaking, I cannot tell if the word is meant as an oath or a prayer." Steiner is dead. "He could not have lived long after tumbling," Murphy says, "The bullet ripped an artery in his throat."[157]

"Following the delay, the Can-Do [15th] Regiment moved through San Marcos, San Felice, and Durrazano, reaching Veccaria near the Volturno River on October 6."[158] It is about this point, in early October, that Corporal Murphy recalls a somewhat lighter encounter with the enemy. "At dusk," he wrote, "we halt in a grove, with orders to dig in. Novak's prowling eyes discover a haystack." Murph and Novak proceed to gather hay from the stack, hoping to make the night's rest a bit more comfortable. They hear muffled voices coming from the other side of the stack. As they are about to leave, two figures appear from the other side, and let out a curse--in German. "For an instant," he continues, "the four of us stand stupidly sharing a mutual paralysis of surprise. Then, clutching our straw, we take off. If those two Germans ran any faster than we, they must have broken track records."[159]

"Within six more days [after the fall of Naples] Allied troops had advanced to the Volturno, twenty miles north of Naples, where exhaustion and a stubborn German defense brought them to a halt... One hundred and fifty feet in width and ranging from three to six feet in depth, the Volturno was well protected by strongly defended German emplacements on the north side."[160] It was here that Simpson tells us that, "Audie and four members of 'B' Company, several days before the crossing, set up and maintained a forward observation post in an abandoned German dugout on the south bank of the river. Their orders were to 'hold until relieved.'"[161] Murph remembers that time in *To Hell and Back*. "The rain fell in a steady drizzle when we reached the banks of the Volturno River," he writes. "It is early night when we creep up to a dugout built by the enemy. It is supposed to be abandoned. But Kerrigan is not sure. He is a stickler for front-line courtesy. Before entering strange places, he first sends in his favorite calling card, a sputtering grenade." These men have learned the hard way that it is always better to play such situations safe.[162]

They are part of a decoy. The main

forces will cross elsewhere. The men are resigned to the job, commenting that at least they aren't getting wet. Early on the first morning, Cpl. Murphy goes out of the cave to check the terrain. "I see a curious shrub in a thicket," he recalls, "Its leaves seem to be turned the wrong way." Sure enough, the days he spent hunting squirrels and rabbits to feed his family, and that "mystical rapport with nature" he shares with the heroes of myth, have paid off. When he fires toward the shrub, a barrage of small arms fire sends him back inside the cave. The patrol members spend their time inside the cave with such pastimes as betting on who has the most fleas, and ragging Antonio, an Italian-American whose romantic dreams of seeing his homeland have faded with the rain and mud. But by the third day, their situation grows desperate. They have run out of water, and their thirst is almost unbearable. The squad leader reassures his men, "Relief will come today. Headquarters knows our situation." But Antonio has had it. "You can take Italy and ram it," he says in disgust. "To hell with it. To hell with everything." Within a few hours, Antonio will be dead, giving his life in an attempt to bring water back to the men who had "ragged" him.[163] It is only a matter of hours afterward that relief finally comes. The next day they cross the Volturno and head for Mignano.[164]

  On Tuesday, October 19, Captain

Butcher observed in his journal, "Military operations are going well but slowly. Heavy rains have hindered effective use of our air and have bogged down our ground troops. However, they have crossed the Volturno River and are pushing slowly ahead on the road to Rome."[165]

"By the end of October, the 3rd and the 34th Infantry Divisions stand poised at the southern entrance to the Mignano Gap, a narrow, six mile long, north-south corridor dominated by numerous sharp peaks, including Mount Rotundo, Mount Lungo, Mount Camino, and Mount Casino."[166] It is at Mignano that Corporal Murphy and his companions experience one of the stranger ironies of civilized warfare.

"In the valley the battle grows in intensity," he writes. "Several times we try storming up the southern side of Mt. Rotundo and are stopped cold...Barrages of artillery and mortar fire are thrown upon us. Groups are isolated. Lines become confused."[167] By nightfall, Corporal Murphy and his companions manage to find an abandoned quarry on "Hill 193." At dawn, they spot a German combat patrol. They open fire. Four of the seven Germans surrender. The other three are severely wounded. One member of the squad takes the healthy prisoners back to headquarters. The rest, including Murph, carry out a bizarre duty. They spend the next several days watching the wounded prisoners die. "The peculiar ethics of war," he writes, "condone our riddling the bodies with lead. But then they were soldiers. Swope's gun has transformed them into human beings again, and the rules say that we cannot leave them unprotected against a barrage of their own artillery." And that German artillery barrage grows stronger, the rain continues to fall harder. The Germans wounds are too severe for them to recover, especially without medics or medication, neither of which is available. "Since there is no hope for life," Murph reports, "we wish these men would die quickly." In the meantime, they make their enemies as comfortable as they can and wait.[168] According to Murphy's friend, David "Spec" McClure, during this incident Murphy, "took off his own coat and placed it over [the] dying enemy soldier to shield him against the driving rain. The act was typical. Although ruthless in combat, he could not kill men who had no chance to defend themselves."[169]

Artillery. The word alone is enough to make the men dash for cover. Before the war started, Audie thought it would be noble, the pitting of one man against the other in armed combat. And in earlier wars, perhaps it was, but the advancements in technological weaponry during the 20th Century have made the "nobility" seem ludicrous. Even in the earliest days of Murph's war he wondered,

"How do you pit skill against skill if you cannot even see the enemy?"[170] In the book, *Iron John*, by Robert Bly, a study of the predicament of the modern male, the author writes that, "Contemporary war, with its mechanical and heartless destruction, has made the heat of aggression seem disgraceful. Ares is not present on the contemporary battlefield."[171] The enemy during World War II was often faceless. And in spite of his outstanding courage in battle, Audie Murphy would continue to fight that faceless enemy, over and over again, in his dreams, for the rest of his life.

The men in Murph's Division, at this point, were pushing their limit of endurance, but they continued to fight with great courage. "In early November, accompanied by the thunder of massed artillery pieces, American troops began their push thorough the Mignano Gap. German resistance was fierce. Enemy forces on the hilltop brought accurate fire to bear on the attackers with an intensity rarely seen in World War II."[172] In a couple of weeks, the Division would be relieved, for a much needed rest - in Naples.

3
Naples
The Meeting with the Goddess

"The 3rd Division came out of the front lines on November 16 and 17, 1943," wrote Harold Simpson.[173] It had been 56 days since they landed at Salerno. In *To Hell and Back*, Murphy recalled that when they were "pulled out of the lines," that they were, "Crawling with mud and sodden with weariness."[174] It is no wonder. The division had been under fire the entire time. During those arduous days, however, Cpl. Murphy had built a reputation not only as a capable leader, but a caring one as well. Murph had known Corliss Rowe, a fellow Texan, since basic training. They had both joined the 3rd Division in North Africa. During a 1974 interview with Simpson, Rowe "remembered when they were fighting in the mountains east and north of Naples that he saw Audie on several occasions carry the pack and guns of members of his squad who could not keep up the pace."[175] Rowe's recollection is not surprising. Audie had been figuratively carrying the load for those weaker than he since early childhood. Now he was doing it literally.

As they trudged away from the lines, Murph reflected, "It is as simple as that. An order comes through, and you are handed life back on a platter"[176] He had learned a lot since leaving Sicily, when he reported in To Hell and Back that he had, "seen war as it actually was." In the book, *Heroes of World War II*, Edward F. Murphy relates that if Sgt. Murphy had any "lingering thoughts...that war was glamorous, Italy totally eliminated them. War was mud, mules, and mountains, not glorious cavalry charges. War was dark nights, rainy days, patrols, and hunger. War was grenades, rifles, and machine guns. But most of all, war was pain and death."[177]

    The 56 days of combat had Murph and his companions so tensed for action that it was hard to believe they were actually walking away from it, even for a short time. Several of them joked that, knowing the Army, they were probably only being called back for a "short arm" inspection and being checked for venereal disease, even though they hadn't seen a single woman during the entire push.[178] Murph had noticed as early as Palermo how, "individual dignity [had] been transformed to fit the nature of war," when he saw, "Lines of soldiers, with their weapons slung over their shoulders, stand before brothels, patiently waiting their turn."[179] Perhaps his buddies, even at the moment, were looking forward to similar services, but our eighteen year-old hero had a higher goal in mind. A camp follower named Drago, who once lived in Naples, now offers Murph the chance to meet a "nice" girl named Maria. The price will not be too high: a few cans of C-rations for her hungry family, and cigarettes, which he didn't smoke anyway, will get him an invitation to dinner with her family.[180]

"The idea of an actual girl sets my brain afire," he remembers, "As I lie in my blankets at night, she comes to me from the darkness. A tiny brunette with chestnut hair tumbling to her shoulders. She is delicate as a flower, and beautiful as June..."[181]

Joseph Campbell would recognize the image. In *Hero with a Thousand Faces* he writes of the "Goddess" that the hero encounters during his dark journey. "She is the paragon of all paragons of beauty, the reply to all desire, the bliss-bestowing goal of every hero's earthly and unearthly quest." Campbell continues saying that each individual hero's vision of his particular "soul-mate" begins with his mother.[182] Audie Murphy's mother fit that physical description when she was young. So will nearly every woman in his life ahead who becomes important to him.

When newly promoted Sgt. Murphy meets his real Maria, she is not quite what he had dreamed of, and a German air raid interrupts the festivities with her family. But he spends the evening with the girl in her darkened living room, listening to the whistle and explosions of the bombs. As the evening goes on, he writes, "her fingertips move through my hair. A rugged pom-pom of the ack-ack begins again on the fringes of the city. For a moment I visualize the pips dancing on the scope of a radar instrument; the strained eyes of men, who are swiftly, deftly plotting the fire range; the tired, cursing gunners returning to their positions of action. Then I fall into a sleep that is not haunted by dreams."[183]

    Murph's dreamless nights will not last long. Already plans are being made that will take him even deeper into the "dark night journey of the soul" that was World War II.

4
ANZIO
The Lesson of Futility

"It all started in an atmosphere of fine cognac and good cigars, this Anzio thing," wrote Fred Sheehan in *Anzio: Epic of Bravery*. Before it was over, the situation at Anzio would prove to illuminate Joseph Campbell's description of the increasingly dark nature of the adventure, which, "after the first thrills of getting underway," he wrote, "develops into a journey of darkness, horror, disgust, and phantasmagoric fears."[184]

After the 3rd Division was pulled from the Italian Front at Mignano, Clark's 5th Army stalemated. In mid-November, he halted the attack and withdrew to regroup and replan. When Kesselring pulled some of his forces to slow down Montgomery's advance, he tried again. For the first two weeks of December, the 36th Division tried to break through at San Pietro. They suffered extremely heavy casualties.[185]

The stalemate could in no way be attributed to the lack of skill or valor on the part of the soldiers. The entire warrior-hero concept that developed during the ten millennia of the Agricultural Era of human existence was being challenged by the technology that developed out of the Industrial Revolution that occurred over a hundred years earlier. The mechanization of combat that the foot soldier faced was compounded by the technological improvements in transportation and communication that allowed major decisions to be made by armchair "generals" who never saw the battlefield. The debacle at Anzio is a prime example. On the German side, Adolph Hitler saw what he had in Albert Kesselring as he forced the Allies to give up time and lives on their push from Salerno, and put the decisions in his hands. According to William Allen, "When the Fuhrer placed his confidence in Kesselring instead of Rommel, the major battles of the Rapido River and at Anzio became inevitable."[186]

Basically, the idea of an Anzio landing consisted of making an "end run" behind the German lines to divert some of Kesselring's forces from the Gustav line, and provide support for a push toward Rome. Eisenhower, Alexander, and Clark first considered the possibility during November on the condition there would be a time when, "the landing force and main army could be mutually supporting," according to Morison.[187]

The preliminary planning for what would be Operation SHINGLE was entrusted to Mark Clark. Anzio was selected as the landing point. It was at that time that Truscott's 3rd Army was pulled from the front for a period of rest and intensive training. However, when the allied advance against the Gustav line stalled, the plan was abandoned. Truscott's division was to return to the line and cross the Rapido below Cassino. Truscott was working on the plans for this assault when the Big Three Conference met in Teheran at the end of November. As a result of that meeting, Operation SHINGLE was on again. Meanwhile, Truscott and Clark were still planning their attack on the Gustav line as late as Christmas Day, 1943.[188]

    On Dec 28, Clark informed Truscott that the 3rd would be landing at Anzio after all. Truscott was not pleased. He felt the timing was wrong, that his men wouldn't have enough time to train properly for the landing. He insisted on a dry run. The staged invasion was a shambles. Still, the landing was scheduled. The 3rd Division would land at Anzio on January 22. The success of the landing would depend on Mark Clark's ability to get through the Gustav line in time to provide support and divert the forces directed at the beachhead.[189]

    Captain Butcher's journal entry for January 16 reads: "Ike found the PM [Churchill] insistent that the SHINGLE operation, the end run to Anzio toward Rome...be executed...despite shortage of landing craft and the great hazard of annihilation to the landing force if the Fifth Army should be unable to reach it by land. General Clark told me he wanted his ground forces at Frosinone before the end run is attempted."[190]

Meanwhile, the soldiers of the 3rd were completely in the dark as to where they would be going after their rest and retraining at Naples. "Night and day we spend hours executing tactics against a supposed enemy," Sgt. Murphy writes, "the men are in a dark mood. They are certain we are being prepared for slaughter. Rumors buzz. We are spearheading an assault on a new beachhead. We are to invade southern France. We are to be sent to England for a cross-channel D-Day. And despite the amphibious training, some say we are to lead an all-out drive to Rome."[191]

As the date approached closer, Murphy recalled the staged invasion: "Naval artillery pounds the shore. The barrage lifts. We leap from landing craft and falling, crawling, firing, advance upon assigned objectives." Then the maneuvers suddenly stop. "We know the signs," he writes, "'Tomorrow' is on everyone's lips." As things turned out, "tomorrow" for Sgt. Murphy meant a trip to the infirmary. His recurrent malaria had flared up again. He had tried to hide it. "I lacked the guts to be called a coward," he explained.[192]

While Murph was being treated in a hospital in Naples, the initial landing went well. As Edward Murphy reported in *Heroes of WWII*, "By noon the British had pulled two miles inland, the Americans, three. By the end of the day over thirty-six thousand troops were ashore." But the positive landing results were not to last long, as he continues, "Field Marshal Kesselring reacted swiftly to this new threat. By nightfall three fresh German divisions were headed south from Northern Italy. Elements of four more divisions were withdrawn from Monte Cassino...By the end of the fourth day Kesselring had nearly eight divisions ringing Anzio. Five more were on their way."[193] The Anzio commander, Major General John Lucas, did not want to push inland until he had more men and supplies ashore. At this point, he had only moved ten miles inland. Lucas had been concerned about the plan from the beginning. He wanted more time. The plan's success depended on Mark Clark's men getting there in time to reinforce them.[194] In later years, the major blame for the debacle that was to follow would be placed on Lucas' shoulders, but on January 20, when Clark tried to attack across the Rapido River, he failed. "Through torrential rain the Corps strove to keep supplies coming up," wrote Morison. "Casualties mounted, the push slowed down, and after two bloody days the Rapido bridgehead was abandoned on the very day of the Anzio landings. All of the valor and energy of this attack went for naught." Morison would conclude that, "Defeat on the Rapido doomed the Anzio beachhead to a long stalemate, if not to failure," and that, "If blame there be, Generals Clark and Alexander must share it with General Lucas."[195]

In the meantime, Sgt. Murphy, recovering from his bout with malaria, joined his company on the beachhead. He arrived in time to lead a night reconnaissance patrol into the German lines, and to learn that one of his closest friends has died. "A spasm of loneliness seizes me," he wrote, "I am not one to question the way of things, but, almighty God, why did it have to be Little Mike?" Mike Novak was a fictionalized version of Murph's friend Joe Sieja.[196] When the war finally ended, Murphy would write the book *To Hell and Back* about his experiences and dedicate the book to two of his lost buddies. Joe Sieja was one of those buddies.

Lucas ordered an attack on the Alban Hills on Jan 30. According to Fred Sheehan, "Far to the east and simultaneous with the British attack, the U. S. 3rd Division began to probe around Cisterna...General Truscott ordered an attack in force...the 15th Infantry attacking on the right along the Canca-Cisterna road."[197] The attack did not succeed, but Morison feels that Lucas was not remiss in holding off the push into the Alban Hills. "He showed sound tactical sense in making consolidations of the beachhead paramount. He knew that the Germans were past masters at cutting off flying columns and pinching out salients. If Lucas had 'stuck his neck out,' he would in all probability have lost his neck, and the beachhead, too."[198]

The 15th Regiment started up the road toward Cisterna during the early morning hours of January 30. Murph and his men are prepared for the coming attack. They begin to move forward, "Fear is moving up with us," writes Murphy, "It always does...." He says he is, "well acquainted with fear," and goes on to explain how "it strikes first in the stomach, coming like a disemboweling hand that is thrust into the carcass of a chicken. I feel now as though icy fingers have reached into my mid-parts and twisted the intestines into knots."[199] Years later he would speak often about fear, that it was a natural instinct we should not be ashamed of. "I was scared before every battle." Harold Simpson would later report him as saying, "That old instinct of self-preservation is a pretty basic thing, but while the action was going on some part of my mind shut off and my training and discipline took over and I would do what I had to do."[200]

William Allen describes the situation faced by Sgt. Murphy and his men. "German machine gunners set up in the several farmhouses pinned down the advancing Americans, and an enemy self-propelled gun knocked out four of the accompanying tanks of the 751st tank Battalion. Before additional armor could be brought up, German Infantry advanced down the hidden streambed from Isola Bella and drove back the outposts along the 15th's right flank. Intermittent firefights continued throughout the remainder of the day across the 3rd Division front."[201]

The moments just before the battle begins are the worst, according to Murph. "It will be far better when the guns open up." He explains. "The nerves will relax, the heart stop its thumping. The brain will turn to animal cunning. The job is directly before us: Destroy and survive."[202]

Not too many years before his death, Murphy told a reporter, Harold B. Morgan, "...the first shock of combat numbs your senses.... You realize you are going to do what you have to do.... The enemy is very impersonal...just a number of people in uniform trying to kill you. So all you can do is develop the mental attitude of an executioner, and get on with it."[203] It is easier to understand the necessity of his detachment when you read his account in *To Hell and Back* of what happens next: "...all hell erupts. From a dozen points come bursts of automatic fire. Branches and leaves clipped from trees rain amid the whizzing steel." He continues, "A scream rises from a wounded man, but the noise is lost in the whistle of an oncoming shell."[204] The German artillery begins a massive barrage. Reinforcements cannot reach them. They cannot retreat.[205]

During the battle, a sniper begins firing at Murph's platoon. Prompting a soldier named

Mason to remark, "that sonofabitch. Think I'll walk over and twist his goddamned ears off." Moments later, Mason is dead, killed by the concussive force of an incoming shell. Murphy recalls,

> Briefly a picture trembles in my mind. It is of a white-haired woman standing before a cottage on a shady street in Savannah.
>
> "I am his mother," she says, "what were his last words?"
> "Said, 'Think I'll go over and twist his goddamned ears off.'"
> "Whose ears?"
> "Those of a German soldier trying to kill us."
> "My boy went to his God with a curse on his lips?"
> "His God will understand."[206]

Finally, they withdraw for a sleepless night. Two Ranger battalions had been trapped just south of Cisterna. The remaining Rangers and the 15th Regiment try, the next day, to reach them.[207] "Tired and irritated beyond measure, we wake in a savage mood. The madness of battle grows within us. So does our indifference to life and death." But the were not able to reach the Rangers, and 803 of them were lost, "in one day at one point along one road at Anzio."[208] Another day: the 15th attacks again. "Like robots driven by coiled springs, we again move forward.... Repeatedly we get the signal to advance.... The big guns have zeroed in. Living now becomes a matter of destiny, or pure luck."[209]

Earlier in *To Hell and Back*, as Murph and his companions were leaving the front in mid-November, he had written that, "Hill 193 will be but another small rise in Italy's rugged terrain."[210] It was at Hill 193 that Murphy's patrol had encountered those "peculiar ethics of war" that led to their three-day stay with a group of dying German soldiers, rather than leave them at the mercy of their own artillery. That WWII artillery serves as an example of how increased technology has affected the honor of combat. There is a vast difference between individual men striving hand-to-hand and the emotionless machinery of modern warfare. The "rules of good conduct" seem hopelessly antiquated. For example, as Murphy continues to write of this battle, "The medics are as bloody as butchers. Unarmed and with plainly marked helmets, they are supposed to be spared by the Germans. But the projectiles have no eyes. And I see one fall dead on a man whose wounds he was dressing. A scrap of metal severed his backbone."[211]

Murphy's battalion moved slowly, but finally gained it's first day objective, a mile from Cisterna,[212] but with the Germans reinforced, the second straight day of attack is worse than the first; artillery is joined by intensive small arms fire. "We kill men by the score..." he writes, "But always, when we come into range, a cyclone of automatic fire sweeps through our ranks." Still, they try again. "All afternoon we throw ourselves against the enemy....Again, we are forced to withdraw." And on the third day, they renew their attack, moving along the Cisterna-Littorio Rd,[213] "Staggering with weariness and snarling like wolves." But again the GIs are repelled. Finally, that night, they fall back, ordered to dig in to the original beachhead. "Some of the companies have been reduced to twenty men," wrote the eighteen-year-old sergeant. "Not a yard of ground has been gained by the murderous three days of assault."[214] General Clark tells Lucas to call off the attack.[215] During the three days of battle, the Allies have suffered fifty-five hundred casualties.[216]

"LONDON, WEDNESDAY, FEBRUARY 9, 1944," begins Harry Butcher's entry for the day, "The Italian campaign has bogged down, leaving the armchair strategists who were overenthusiastic when the beachhead landings went so well now are equally overpessimistic. Apparently these wiseacres now seek a 'goat' on whom to lay the failure to exploit our initial advantage."[217]

William Allen gives an account of life on

Anzio for the next several months, from March to May: "They seemed to be living on an island rather than a beachhead.... There was no rear area to rest in, no rear echelon, no safe place to unload the thousands of tons of supplies."[218]

"When the Allies failed to crack the iron German ring that hemmed in the beachhead," wrote David McClure, "the soldiers were ordered to dig in and hold at all costs. 'It was the only time during the war that I felt we were all doomed,' says Murphy. 'I cannot explain it. But doom seemed to be everywhere I turned; in the rain that filled our foxholes; in the mud that sucked at our feet; in the howling wind; in the eyes of the men; and in the very light of day'"[219]

Seeing women during wartime is a rarity for the fighting GI. It is not surprising that Murph took the opportunity, during another bout with malaria, to trade barbs with a pretty nurse named Helen. He is defensive at first, especially when she asks him about home. "We had a lot of kids in the family and needed food," he told her, "So I hunted a lot and learned to shoot straight. I couldn't afford to miss." Realizing that Helen is sympathetic, he softens. "That comes in handy now," he tells her openly. "Sometimes I had just one shell. Sometimes in the field, I dream of walking in the darkness with that one shell. The Germans are all around me, and I know that I don't have the ammo to stand up against them. I wake up with the shakes…"[220] It is hard not to recall, when reading this, of another wartime encounter with a woman: his night in Naples, with Maria, and the bliss of a night of "deep sleep, unhaunted by dreams." Murph left the hospital and returned to the front. It would have been shortly afterward when, as Allen reported, "Doctors, nurses, and patients died when long range artillery--and bombing--missed their targets."[221] Sgt. Murphy heard of the bombings. "I try," he wrote, "but never find out whether Helen was among those who got it."[222]

"Along the perimeter," Allen writes, "the troops had only shallow foxholes for protection. Water rose in holes only two feet deep, and overhead protection of some kind was needed for protection against shell fragments."[223] As Murphy tells it, "Rain is slanting in black streaks, turning our area into a sea of mud. It pulls at our feet like quicksand…. For hours we crouch in ankle-deep water."[224] But he keeps up a front for his friends back home. He doesn't want them to worry, so he writes to Beatrice "Pete" Springfield, "We have been having some nasty weather here it rains almost every nt and when you dig a hole it becomes a bath tub full of water! the only catch is the water is cold and you have no way to drain the damn thing. no plug to pull no fancy spout just take a can and bail her out…"[225]

In *To Hell and Back*, he uses a very different tone: All they can do is, "…listen to the roar of the wind, curse our existence, and snarl at one another. There is no escape with honor," he wrote, "except on the litter of the medics or in the sack of the burial squads."[226]

But Sgt. Murphy's attitude does not impair his fighting ability. It is during this stalemate that Sgt. Murphy wins his first medal for valor. Apparently, one advantage of the rain and mud is that it has prevented the advance of German tanks. As bad as the rain and mud is, the men become anxious over breaks in the weather. As Murphy recalls one such break, at his lookout post in the upstairs room of a bombed-out house, he spots a German tank, then twenty tanks. Sgt. Murphy grabs a phone and a map, and begins calling coordinates to his own artillery. One tank is disabled and the rest turn back. But Murph is concerned about the disabled tank. It could be repaired, so the young sergeant gathered a volunteer patrol and they set off after the tank. He related the story in a *Dallas Times Herald* article during the summer of 1945. "I left my men in a ditch 200 yards from it and crawled slowly through the mud toward the tank.

"I was afraid to make any noise. No, that's not right. I was just plain afraid. Anyone who tells you he isn't scared in a spot like that is a liar. I was wishing my shirt didn't have any buttons so I could get closer to the ground." He tried two Molotov cocktails, to no avail. He tried a hand grenade. It didn't work much better. He then worked his way backwards just enough to fire two rifle grenades, disabling the tank permanently. "The Nazis didn't like that.," Murph continued. "They opened fire from all directions, converging on the tank and it's immediate vicinity. I could see the tracers criss-crossing a few inches from the ground not nearly far enough away.

"I didn't worry about making noise then. I jumped up and got out of there – probably the fastest 200 yard dash in history"[227] His actions are described in the citation for his first Bronze Star:

> On the night of 2 March 1944, on the ANZIO BEACHHEAD in Italy, First Lieutenant [then Staff Sergeant] MURPHY crept 100 yards over flat, open terrain during a fire fight between his small patrol and a group of Germans, to a point 50 yards from a partly disabled enemy tank. Taking careful aim, he fired several rifle grenades at the tank, hitting and completely destroying it. Then, when a great many enemy machine guns in the sector opened up, he led his men through bullet swept area to safety.[228]

The action was the first in a long line of

corroborated incidents that indicate Murph's sense of responsibility to others was growing stronger during the war. His main concern was never his own safety, but that of his men. When he told David McClure of the tank incident, he said, "If I discovered one valuable thing during my early combat days, it was audacity, which is often mistaken for courage or foolishness. It is neither. Audacity is a tactical weapon. Nine times out of ten it will throw the enemy off-balance and confuse him."[229]

"Finally," wrote Edward Murphy in *Heroes of WWII*, following four weeks of massive preparation, the Fifth Army launched an all-out determined attack. Beginning on May 11, tens of thousands of Allied soldiers hit the Gustav line. Slowly, foot by bloody foot, the Germans were pushed back. By May 17, British troops had pushed far through the Liri Valley to flank Cassino and the monastery. The Germans withdrew. On May 18, Monte Cassino fell to Polish troops. By May 23, Kesselring's Tenth Army was in retreat all along the main battlefront."[230]

At Anzio, the weather improves, and so do the spirits of Sgt. Murphy: "Spring comes to the beachhead, and on the ruined land new green glistens in the sunlight," he writes. And as Kesselring retreats from Monte Cassino, on May 23, Murph and the rest of the 3rd begin a massive attack. He writes, "...Under the spinning shells we turn from the holes in which we have cowered ourselves for nearly four months and march toward the enemy."[231]

Fred Sheehan describes the situation. "The riflemen of the 3rd Division and 1st Special Force climbed slowly out of their holes and crept forward, then begin a crouching run as their heavy machine guns spit out a covering fire…. Backed by tanks and tank destroyers, the 3rd Division opened a two-pronged assault against Cisterna, to encircle the town, then reduce it."[232] Company B's objective is the railroad track running to the south of the town. Murph and his platoon head down a deep cut. "He was almost killed," wrote McClure, "when his trench shovel caught on a rock and hung him up on a railway bank. An enemy machine gunner spotted him and started zeroing in. The bullets were hitting so close that Audie could smell the rock dust they kicked up."[233] Sgt. Murphy recounted the same incident in *To Hell and Back*. "I free myself with a desperate heave and bolt across the tracks." Chided by an anxious buddy for almost getting himself killed, Murph replied sarcastically, "I was interested in the scenery."[234]

"At seven-thirty on the morning of May 25 on the road southwest of Borgo Grappa," wrote Sheehan, "First Lt. Francis X. Buckley of the II Corps 48th Engineer Combat Battalion extended his hand to his fellow engineers of the 36th Combat Regiment…and Anzio ceased to be a beachhead. Thus ended four months and three days of isolation."[235]

Butcher's journal entry for May 29th seems significant. "In Italy the Eighth and Fifth Armies have been giving Kesselring's Tenth Army a good beating. The main front has teamed up with the bridgehead. I saw today for the first time in some days a report of casualties in Italy, ...Total casualties to May 25 are 109,054 and for the Allied beachhead force 33,241. These seem alarmingly high."[236]

General Clark, smarting from the length of the stalemate and the time and men lost during the past months, planned to make up for it all with a triumphal entry into the city of Rome. To ensure that his army would be the first to arrive, he split VI Corps into three groups headed for Rome, with only the 3rd division to secure the strategically important town of Valtomonte. Truscott was displeased. The change in plans would involve a massive switching around of men and materiel, but had no choice except to go along. On May 30, the 3rd Division was taken from Truscott's VI and moved into the II Corps to push on Valtomonte. Sheehan reports that "...by June 3, the II Corps had pushed along the Via Casilina through San Cesarea to Osteria Finocchio, only ten miles from Rome."[237] But Clark's victory was somewhat hollow, since Kesselring pulled out of the city before they arrived. Rome may have had some emotional significance, but was of little political value. The war in Italy was not over.

Murph's attitude reflects what most of the men felt about it. "Rome is but another objective on an endless road called war," he wrote. The futility of the months at Anzio had taken their toll on our hero. Even though they were pulled from the front and sent to garrison Rome, he could not lift himself out of his detachment. He wrote, "We prowl through Rome like ghosts, finding no satisfaction in anything we see or do. I feel like a man briefly reprieved from death; and there is no joy within me. We can have no hope until the war is ended. Thinking of the men on the fighting front, I grow lonely on the streets of Rome."[238]

5
France
The "Nadir" of the Journey

Between the days of July 13-16, The 3rd Division left Rome and began training near Naples; on August 8, they left Italy for the South of France.[239] Where they were going, and why, was explained by Edward F. Murphy, in *Heroes of WWII*: "While Allied troops were still struggling through Normandy's murderous hedgerow country, a second invasion of France took place. On August 15, 1944, Operation ANVIL put ashore ninety-four thousand troops on the shore of the French Riviera at St. Tropez, GI's of the 3rd, 36th, and 45th Infantry Divisions came ashore at the famed resort beaches beginning at 8:00 a.m."[240]

The Landing at Ramatuelle

"Technically it was called a perfect operation," begins Sgt. Murphy's own account of the landing in *To Hell and Back*. "The vast operation designed to crack the enemy coastal defenses…moved with the smooth precision of a machine."[241] Like all mindless machines, this technically perfect operation has no awareness or concern that Sgt. Murphy is about to face one of the most devastating, and at the same time, one of the most courageous days of his life so far. "...We do not know," he continues, "we do not see the gigantic pattern of the offensive...." Their eyes are focused on the portion of the beach where they are to land. They have done this many times before, and always, it has been the same. As the landing boats churn toward the shore and the enemy fire, "...the old fear," he writes, "grapples with my guts." As he has in the past, Murph puts that fear away somewhere in a corner of his mind, and cuts it off. The landing proceeds. They leap from the landing craft. Murph writes, "from the hills the German guns begin to crack....The medics roll up their sleeves and get busy." It will be a typical day for the medics as well as the soldiers. Amid the explosions, Murph writes, "When the smoke lifts I see the torn body of a man who has stepped on a mine. A medic bends over him, rises, and signals four litter bearers that their services will not be needed."[242] The mindless machine progresses. In an article he wrote for the *Dallas Times Herald* shortly after returning to Texas after the war, he described his situation. "As my rifle platoon and I moved inland from the beach, we were halted by machine gun fire from a rocky ridge ahead of us. We dropped to the ground and crawled quickly to cover.

"There was only one thing to do, and I couldn't ask my men to do it."[243] In later years he told a friend, David McClure, how he felt at that moment. "I knew it was going to be a duel to the death between me and the enemy machine gun crew. God! What a lonely feeling."[244] What happened next is described in objective detail in the citation that will accompany the Distinguished Service Cross that he will be awarded for the day's proceedings.

Landing near Ramatuelle, France, with the first wave of the assault infantry, at 0800 hours, 15 August until halted by intense machine gun and small arms fire from a boulder-covered hill to their front. Leaving his men in a covered position, he dashed forty yards through withering fire to a draw. Using this defiladed route, he went back toward the beaches, found a light machine gun squad and, returning up the rocky hill, placed the machine gun in position seventy-five yards in advance of his platoon. In the duel which ensued, Lieutenant Murphy silenced the enemy weapon, killed two of the crew and wounded a third. As he proceeded further up the draw, two Germans advanced toward him. Quickly destroying both of them, he dashed up the draw alone toward the enemy strongpoint, disregarding bullets which glanced off the rocks around him and hand grenades which exploded fifteen yards away. Closing in, he wounded two Germans with carbine fire, killed two more in a fierce, brief fire-fight, and forced the remaining five to surrender. His extraordinary heroism resulted in the capture of a fiercely contested enemy-held hill and the annihilation or capture of the entire enemy garrison.[245]

The citation leaves out what would have been the most important part of the story to Murph. Looking around, he notices that Lattie Tipton (Brandon, in the autobiography) has joined him. "Lattie and I had shared foxholes ever since the invasion of Sicily," he recalled in the *Dallas Times Herald* article, "He had turned down a sergeant's rating so he could stay with me as my runner."[246] Together they work their way up. After they throw a grenade into a machine gun nest, the Germans raise a white flag. Lattie stands up. "I hear the clash of machine gun fire," he wrote in *To Hell and Back*. "As Brandon [Lattie] topples back into the pit, he softly mutters 'Murph.'" With that one word, his closest friend dies in his arms. He refuses to believe what has happened. "He is not dead," he continues. "He can't be dead, because if he is dead, the war is all wrong; and Brandon has died in vain."[247] At that point, for the first time, his rage overcomes his reason, and he grabs a weapon, and charges the hill single-handedly. "I must have gone crazy then," he wrote in the summer of '45. "I remember using a German machine gun I picked up somewhere, maybe from the Kraut whose lower jaw had been shot to bits, and every time he tried to scream a stream of blood spurted out. I wish I didn't remember that." Soon, the hill is completely cleared of the enemy and Murph returns to the spot where Lattie lies dead and sits down beside him. "I open his purse and take a last look at the little girl with the pigtails…Then I sit by his side and bawl like a baby."[248] As Edward F. Murphy would later write, "Murphy would receive the DSC on March 5, 1945 for this deed, but it never made up for the loss of his buddy. 'I won the DSC' he said, but all he got was death.'"[249]

"SHELLBURST [IN NORMANDY], TUESDAY, AUGUST 15, 1944
Beetle, Admiral Ramsey, and Lieutenant General 'Pug' Ismay came to dinner...General De Witt and his aide were already here, so there were eight for dinner....We have just heard from Major General Alexander M. Patch...who commands the U. S. Seventh Army in the southern landings. He says the operation seems successful.

"Our old friend Lucian Truscott is commanding the VI Corps, which is comprised of the 3rd, 36th, and 45th Divisions, which were the assault divisions...All the assault divisions reported successful breaching of beach defenses in target area and the attack was proceeding according to plan."[250]

Montelimar
(*The Face in the Mirror*)

The 3rd Division began its march through Southern France. "On August 28, Free French troops completed the capture of Marseilles, the Riviera's major port. From there, the invasion's commander, Lt. Gen. Lucian Truscott, sent his troops up National Highway 7 along the Rhone River toward Montelimar.... Pausing only long enough to refuel or crush small German garrisons. Truscott's troops moved even faster than Patton's troops in Normandy."[251]

At Montelimar an incident occurred that Murph would never forget. His company entered Montelimar on August 28 to secure the town. He entered a house, not knowing if it contained Germans or not, and proceeded cautiously until he saw, "a terrible looking creature with a tommy gun. His face is black, his eyes are red and glaring." Murph and the creature appear to fire simultaneously, at which point, the image shatters. "The horrible being that I shot," he wrote, "was the reflection of my own smoke-blackened face in a mirror.

Kerrigan doubles with laughter. 'That's the first time I ever saw a Texan beat himself to the draw,' says he."[252] Although the incident is treated lightly in the book, it has a mythological significance that was not lost on Murph. It impressed itself on his mind so strongly that it was one of the first things he wrote about when he returned to the States at the war's end.[253]

A similar incident, mythologically speaking, occurred in George Lucas' second Star Wars movie, "The Empire Strikes Back." Luke Skywalker goes into a dark cave, where he sees the image of his enemy, Darth Vader.[254] He strikes the figure a blow with his light saber, and Vader's helmeted head is lopped off and lands at his feet. At that moment, the mask disintegrates, and Luke finds himself staring at his own face. Later in the movie, shortly after the moment that Vader has lopped off Luke's hand with his light saber, Luke learns that his hated enemy is his own father. Eventually he comes to terms with this knowledge, and in "Return of the Jedi," is determined to save his father, convinced him that there is still good in him.[255] Toward the end of this third and final movie of the series, drawn into a battle with Vader by the emperor, Luke shears off his father's hand, and sees that it, like his own, is a mechanical replacement. At this moment, he realizes that no matter how evil his father might have been, to kill him would be to kill himself, and he refuses to allow the emperor to goad him any further.

Campbell refers to this realization as coming to an "Atonement with the Father." In the earliest societies, when a boy reached the appropriate age, he was taken from his mother by his father, and initiated into the world of men[256], as Audie's father had done when the boy was five years old, taking him into the fields to learn the ways of farming. According to Campbell, the mythological father is supposed to be "the guide and initiator to the mysteries of the unknown. As the original intruder into the paradise of the infant with its mother, [he] is the archetypal enemy; hence, throughout life all enemies are symbolical (to the unconscious) of the father." Because of the child's reluctance to leave the safety his mother provides, there is "a new element of rivalry in the picture: the son against the father for the mastery of the universe."[257] Since Murph's relationship with his own father was such a negative one, that rivalry would naturally be intense.

Campbell continues, referring to studies by Geza Roheim, "Whatever is killed becomes the father," and from this crisis arises "the irresistible impulse to make war: The impulse to destroy the father is continually transforming itself into public violence." Eventually, if the hero is to conquer the dark forces, he must become aware of this unconscious projection. "He beholds the face of the father," Campbell writes, "understands--and the two are atoned."[258] It is important to realize at this point that the "father" Campbell refers to is not merely the individual's personal father. He is speaking, rather, of the archetypal concept of Father we all carry in our own minds. In childhood, that image is often distorted by the child's relationship with his or her personal father. When animosity develops between a father and son, and to a degree, such animosity is inevitable, a child often carries that animosity with him. The lesson learned when he "sees himself in the face of the father," (or the enemy), is that he, too, can commit evil acts under the right circumstances. He is, in that sense, no different from his father, or from the enemy he fights. Marie-Louise von Franz explains Carl Jung's concept of an individual's "Shadow" personality as "all those... inferior aspects that tend to condense in an enemy and are unashamedly projected onto persons in the environment."[259] She also explains how a child whose father or mother is a negative influence will "project" that image onto other people, often not consciously realizing that he or she might be personally repeating those same negative behaviors.[260] In such cases, the Shadow of that individual's personality can become strongly tinged with with the behaviors of the personal father. It is interesting, in that light, to note that Darth Vader of the Star Wars saga is an obvious Shadow figure, and that after

Luke realized that Vader was indeed, his own father, he also realized that to kill his enemy would be the same as killing himself. By coming to such a realization, the hero begins to see through the distortion of the relationship with the personal father, to the archetypal ideal. "I and the father are one" implies not only the acceptance of one's own acts, it clarifies an image of what fatherhood can and ought to be, so that when the hero eventually becomes a father himself, he is not bound to repeat his father's mistakes. It is important, then, for the hero to come to this realization, in order to put the "warrior" archetype to rest. The knowledge gained from seeing oneself in the face of the enemy is one of the most important elements of the message of the returning hero.

It was not only the individual warrior, Audie Murphy, who carried this unconscious projection with him in World War II. All of America was at war with "The Fatherland." And much of our culture is tied up with the language it speaks. The English language itself developed out of Germanic roots, so Germany, in many senses, was a "father" image to the country.

The Vosges Mountains

After the loss of Lattie Tipton, and the realization that he was no different from the enemy he was fighting, all of Sgt. Murphy's being was concentrated on ending the war. From this point, events moved in rapid succession to their final culmination in the end of the journey. By September 6, they had reached Besancon, and headed for Vesoul.

"The French town [of Vesoul] fell on Sept 12, 1944." writes Edward F. Murphy, "By straight line, Vesoul is more than four hundred miles from St. Tropez.... On the same day...soldiers linked up with men from Patton's army near Dijon. A few days later Truscott's Seventh Army was absorbed into Eisenhower's command. Nearly one third of France had been freed. The Allied armies could now concentrate on smashing Hitler's western defenses and driving into Germany."[261] Three days later, Murph is wounded for the first time. But this first wound is not serious. He will spend a few days in the hospital, and return to the front. "Sgt. Murphy rejoined his unit in the front lines on September 27," Simpson reports, "just in time to lead his old platoon in the battle of Cluerie Quarry - one of the bitterest engagements fought by the 15th Infantry during the war."[262] Sometime between Sept 27 and Oct 2, Murph and Kerrigan are patrolling the forest near the quarry when they spot a machine gun nest. Together they go into action. Only Kerrigan misses his shot, and Murph's grenade hit a tree. But in spite of the incident's poor beginning, the five Germans are soon dead.

Murphy tells of the interchange that followed. "'What was wrong, Bo-Peep,' I finally say, 'Have you got a kink in your gun barrel?'" And Kerrigan retorts, "...nice throw you made with the grenade. Like to have you on my ball team." And later, after the two of them trade barbs on everything from their attraction to women to their intellectual abilities, Kerrigan adds, "If you get a commission, I hope you get your ass shot off." A bit later Murph remarks sarcastically, "I'd feel safer if you let me do the shooting and you just throw rocks," and this chapter of *To Hell and Back* ends with the words, "Again the fury of combat closes around us"[263]

The next chapter begins, "Two days later Kerrigan is hit by a mortar shell fragment, but his luck holds out to the end. The sharp steel splinter simply clipped off half his right hand."[264] With Kerrigan out of the action, Murph is the only remaining member of the band of companions that began their journey on the shores of Sicily.

"Though the VI Corps of the Seventh Army had advanced five hundred miles from mid-August through September," Edward F. Murphy writes, "it had made only twenty-five more in October. The supply problem and increasing German resistance slowed the Americans to a snail's pace."[265] "The anchor point of [the German] lines was Cleurie Rock Quarry," wrote David McClure. "Situated on a slope with dense trees, the quarry was honeycombed with tunnels, passages, and walls that protected the krauts against mortar fire." The brunt of the assault was carried out by the 1st Battalion of the 15th Regiment: Murphy's battalion. For four days, his Company B attacked the ridge. "We took and lost that ridge so often that some of the men thought we should be getting flying pay,"[266] Murph later joked to McClure. But the situation wasn't a joke. The frustration of the standoff was particularly upsetting to the young sergeant. Having become obsessed with the war's ending, he did everything he as an individual could do, to hasten it. As a result, he would earn two Silver Stars within three days, and within a week of the second, accept the commission he had turned down so often before.

He earned his first silver star when a group of officers came to see what had been holding the men up, and decided to look into the situation themselves. Sgt. Murphy warned them that it was not a good idea, that they would likely get themselves killed, but they went anyway. Murph later told David McClure of the event. "With grim humor, Murphy picked up a carbine and some grenades to follow the men. 'I figured those gentlemen were going to run into trouble. So I tagged along, about 25 yards to their rear, to watch the stampede.'"[267] What followed is described in the citation that accompanied the medal.

> On the morning of 2 October 1944, near CLEURIE QUARRY, France, First Lieutenant MURPHY inched his way over rugged, uneven terrain, toward an enemy machine gun, which had surprised a group of officers on reconnaissance. Getting to within fifteen yards of the German gun, First Lieutenant MURPHY stood up and, disregarding a burst of enemy fire delivered at such close range and which miraculously missed him, flung two hand grenades into the machine gun position, killing four Germans, wounding three more and destroying the position.[268]

By this time, Murphy's state of mind is one of numbness and depression. "Since Kerrigan got his," he wrote, "I have isolated myself as much as possible, desiring only to do my work and be left alone. I feel burnt out, emotionally and physically exhausted. Let the hill be strewn with corpses so long as I do not have to turn over the bodies and find the familiar face of a friend. It is with the living that I must concern myself, juggling them as numbers to fit the mathematics of battle."[269] He feels little emotion, but a few things do make him angry, most especially the loss of men under his command. He seems to have a special hatred for snipers. It is understandable. In situations where war is honorable, it is a matter of men meeting face to face, but the sniper does his killing in hiding, not giving his enemy a chance. During those days at Cleurie, probably between winning his two Silver Stars, Murph got angry when another sniper killed several of his men. He volunteered to go after him alone. His captain insisted that he take at least two men along, but after a short distance, Murph left them. He doesn't want anyone else dead, and believes that he can sneak up on the sniper more easily if he is alone. He writes, "I and my enemy, it seems, are the last two men on earth. I pause, and fear makes my body grow limp. I look at the hills and sky. A shaft of sunlight pierces the clouds, making the wet leaves of the trees glisten goldenly. Life becomes infinitely desirable." His mind begins to play tricks on him, and the hill appears, "…infested with a thousand eyes peering through telescopic sights, with cross-hairs on the center of my forehead. Terror grows. I crash my fist into my forehead. The fantasy passes." There is little time to worry about the fantasy. "It happens like a flash of lightening," he continues, "There is a rustle. My eyes snap forward. The branches of a bush move. I drop to one knee. We see each other simultaneously. His face is as black as a rotten corpse; and his cold eyes are filled with evil."[270]

This description, whether he consciously realizes it or not, is almost identical to his description of the evil face he had seen in the mirror at Montelimar. He continues his account, "As he frantically reaches for the safety on his rifle, I fire twice. He crashes backwards. I throw two hand grenades...Then I wilt." Perhaps he does see the similarity. As his companions come forward to examine the dead German, he relates, "I suddenly feel like vomiting," and later, "At headquarters I make my report. Then I go to the kitchen, take my carbine apart, and start cleaning it."[271]

Murphy doesn't relate the action that won the second Silver Star in *To Hell and Back*, but the citation describes it clearly.

On the afternoon of 5 October 1944 near LE THOLY, France, First "Lieutenant MURPHY, carrying an SCR 536 radio, crawled fifty yards under severe enemy machine gun and rifle fire, to a point 200 yards from strongly entrenched enemy who had prevented further advance. Despite machine gun and rifle bullets that hit as close as a foot to him, First Lieutenant MURPHY directed artillery fire upon enemy positions for an hour, killing fifteen Germans and inflicting approximately thirty-five additional casualties. His courage, audacity and accuracy enabled his company to advance and attain its objective.[272]

Murphy did recall that action in one of the articles he wrote for the *Dallas Times Herald* during the summer of '45. "It was rainy and dark," he wrote. "and the Krauts were camouflaged and hard to locate, so I grabbed a 536 radio and began crawling.... For an hour I lay there wishing I was a mole. Rifle and machine gun bullets hit as close as a foot from me, but the Nazis couldn't quite get me."[273]

Years after his death, Edward N. Klein would write an article on Murphy's heroism called "Audie Murphy Did A Lot More Than 'Win A Bunch Of Medals'," for the *Hudson Valley Business Journal*. In that article, he would report that "His heroics brought him something he really didn't want: a battlefield promotion to Lieutenant, where he proved that in addition to personal heroism, he was capable of leading others in battle. Seeing him standing in a jeep as we trudged into battle, and hearing his rallying cry when we were ready to run, gave us the stamina we needed to continue."[274]
Murphy finally accepted that promotion on October 14, after he was promised that he would not have to transfer out of his old outfit. Although Murph never wanted to be an officer, reports from men who served under him indicate he was quite capable, even if his appearance surprised some of them at first.

Horace Ditterline remembers his first day in action and being sent to Lt. Murphy's company. "I was scared to death. Murph was just a second lieutenant...and he WAS A LITTLE KID. I mean, actually. He [looked] about 17 and I was 27. And I thought, 'What are YOU doing telling ME what to do?' but I soon got the feeling that he was our company commander and God bless him, I'd do anything I could to help him."[275] Eventually, Pvt. Ditterline came to say that, "If Audie Murphy would have told me to jump off a mountain, I'd have jumped off, 'cause I thought that much of him. Charles Owens, recalling his own first days with Murphy as his commanding officer, indicates why his men though so much of him. "We could hear artillery fire in the distance. And we were wondering what in the world was going to happen to us, you know. Fresh recruits from the states....And he said, 'Now there'll be times when you'll be scared to death. I'm always scared when we're up front. Don't be ashamed of it.' and he said, 'there'll be times when you'll want to cry. There's nothing wrong with that...." Owens went on to say Murph was "different from other officers. He'd sit in a foxhole and just talk to us about personal things. You know, you'd never do that with any other officers. And we'd cover up with the same blanket."[276] Another fellow soldier, retired professor Will Weinberg, told *Entertainment Tonight* that, "If the guys were stuck somewhere, their lives were at stake, or if they were in trouble, in any way, he wouldn't ask questions, he wouldn't wait for an order, he would just go ahead and do it. You could count on that."[277] Two weeks later, he received his second wound. This one was serious. A sniper's ricocheting bullet would tear a long gash in his right hip. "The wound didn't hurt," he wrote for the *Dallas Times Herald*, "It just made me mad. My helmet had fallen off…and the sniper kept firing bullets into it. I was glad I wasn't wearing it."[278] Although he couldn't stand, he was able to kill his assailant before one of his men could reach him. "Kerrigan would get a kick out of this," he told the soldier, "He always said if I took a commission I would get my ass shot off." The soldier replied simply, "Well, you did; and you have."[279]

It would be several days before the medics could get him to a hospital. In the meantime, his wound developed gangrene. He spent a month taking penicillin shots, and having "dead and poisoned flesh" cut away from his hip, and several more weeks recuperating. Before the end, the doctors had cut nine inches of flesh from his right hip, but in the hospital he met two people who would remain long-time friends: a paraplegic named Perry Pitt, and Carolyn Price, a pretty brunette nurse. According to Harold Simpson, he fell in love with "Pricey" and they wrote several letters to each other, and met at least once while he was on leave. He wanted to marry her, but she refused, partly because she was older than he, and partly because he was determined to return to the front.[280] From the hospital, he wrote a letter to Haney Lee, one of the few where he came close to telling anyone back home how he really felt, saying, "either those Krauts are getting to be better shots than they used to be or else my lucks playing out on me and, I guess, someday they will tag me for keeps.... I've seen so much blood I don't think I ever want to shoot anything else..." At this point, all he wanted was to go home, but he did not go home, because he couldn't leave the others behind. "Thares work to be done yet (dirty work)." He wrote in his latter to Haney Lee.[281]

So he returned to the front on January 14, and two weeks later, one day after receiving a third wound, single-handedly saved his entire company, and enabled them to hold their strategic position against over 200 advancing Germans with six tanks.

6
Apotheosis
(The Making of a God)

"Centered on the Alsatian city of Colmar," wrote Edward F. Murphy, "south of Strasbourg, on the eastern slopes of the Vosges, the German bridgehead west of the Rhine poked eighty miles wide and deep into the Allied territory." The 3rd Division was given the job of getting rid of this last pocket of German resistance in France. A two-pronged attack on the Colmar Pocket began Jan 22, with the French I corps moving up from the south and the 3rd Division down from the north. On the 24th, Lt. Murphy's legs were peppered with schrapnel from an exploding shell, but he attended the lacerations himself, and continued fighting. It was a bitterly cold winter. Several inches of snow lay on the ground. The men tried to hack shallow foxholes, but to little avail. The most value they gained from the attempt was that of keeping slightly warmer. On the morning of the 26th, Murph woke to find his hair frozen to the side of his foxhole.[282] He did not know at the time, but his actions this day would soon bring him what Campbell calls the hero's "gift of life."

What happened that morning is reminiscent, in all reports, of the annals of such heroes as Ulysses, King Arthur, and Murphy's fellow Irish hero, the mythical Cuchullain. And it demonstrates, once again, that Murph's heroism was not a self-centered act of a glory seeker who loved battle, but a caring leader wanting only to protect the men in his charge. The fighting had been devastating; some of the worst in the war, and at this point, Lt. Murphy's company had been decimated from nearly 150 down to about twenty men. As the only remaining officer, he had been made company commander. He and his men had been ordered to hold a road leading toward the town of Holtzwihr. Another force was to move up to attack the city, but had been held up. During the early afternoon, Lt. Murphy spotted two reinforced infantry companies and six tanks headed north from the town toward his position. Knowing his men couldn't hold them off; he ordered them back to safety and began calling coordinates to his artillery support.[283] Several pages still exist in Murphy's own handwriting, of his first draft of *To Hell and Back*, and despite their roughness, show an immediacy that is lacking in the other reports of what occurred, including even the finished book. "I direct the artillery, & the first big Barage came in on the nose god, I loved that artillery..." he begins.[284]

This is not the first time Murph tells of directing artillery fire. In two other instances, both of which would lead to medals, he would also be involved in directing such fire. Fellow soldiers from his company later report that he would often call artillery in right over his own head.[285] It is not difficult to understand why he would "love" doing so. Enemy artillery was one of the most frustrating experiences of WWII. The shells would come in from nowhere, and there was nothing the soldier could do to stop it. Directing such fire against the enemy must have given Murphy a sense of control, a feeling desperately needed under the circumstances. In this way, the power was in his hands. He could see the shells hit where he directed them.

  On this particular day, however, even though the artillery was slowing down the enemy advance, especially of the tanks, the infantrymen kept coming. The two tank destroyers that had been assigned to him were both disabled, but he noticed that one of them still had a .50 caliber machine gun intact on its turret. It was also on fire, but that fact did not detain Murph. Carrying the field phone with him, he climbed onto the tank destroyer and began to rake the approaching Germans with it. In between bursts, he continued to call artillery in, closer and closer to his own position, responding to the headquarters lieutenant's anxious questions with humorous barbs. When asked how close the enemy was to his position, he responded, "Hold the phone and I'll let you talk to one of the bastards." When the TD received another direct hit, and Murphy was silent for a moment, the Lt. called over the phone, "Are you still alive?" Murph responded, "I'm fine, what are your post-war plans." Of his own feelings about the action, he wrote, "I am conscious only that the smoke and the turret afford a good cover, and that, for the first time in three days, my feet are warm."[286] The full citation would read

> By direction of the President, under the provisions of the act of Congress approved 9 July 1918 (WD Bul. 43, 1918), a Medal of Honor for conspicuous gallantry and intrepidity at the risk of life above and beyond the call of duty was awarded by the War Department in the name of Congress to the following-named officer: Second Lieutenant Audie L. Murphy, 01692509, 15th Infantry, Army of the United States, on 26 January 1945, near Holtzwihr, France, commanded Company B, which was attacked by six tanks and waves of infantry. Lieutenant Murphy ordered his men to withdraw to a prepared position in a woods while he remained forward at his command post and continued to give fire directions to the artillery by telephone. Behind him to his right one of our tank destroyers received a direct hit and began to burn.

Its crew withdrew to the woods. Lieutenant Murphy continued to direct artillery fire, which killed large numbers of the advancing enemy infantry. With the enemy tanks abreast of his position, Lieutenant Murphy climbed on the burning tank destroyer which was in danger of blowing up any instant and employed its .50 caliber machine gun against the enemy. He was alone and exposed to the German fire from three sides, but his deadly fire killed dozens of Germans and caused their infantry attack to waver. The enemy tanks, losing infantry support, began to fall back. For an hour the Germans tried every available weapon to eliminate Lieutenant Murphy, but he continued to hold his position and wiped out a squad which was trying to creep up unnoticed on his right flank. Germans reached as close as 10 yards only to be mowed down by his fire. He received a leg wound but ignored it and continued the single-handed fight until his ammunition was exhausted. He then made his way to his company, refused medical attention, and organized the company in a counterattack, which forced the Germans to withdraw. His directing of artillery fire wiped out many of the enemy; he personally killed or wounded about 50. Lieutenant Murphy's indomitable courage and his refusal to give an inch of ground saved his company from possible encirclement and destruction and enabled it to hold the woods which had been the enemy's objective.[287]

"I had been on the tank turret for an hour," he wrote for the *Dallas Times Herald*, "and my ammunition was gone. So I dropped over the side and sat down in the snow. I was puzzled: How come I'm not dead?

"After a few minutes of wondering I returned to my company and began reorganizing the attack. We succeeded in clearing the woods and taking the position."[288]

"Around 9 PM on Jan 29, covered by an artillery barrage that blanketed the area with 16,328 rounds of fire, the 7th Infantry, followed closely by the 15th Infantry, started across the Colmar canal," wrote Simpson. After the fall of Colmar, the 3rd was assigned to the "Watch on the Rhine" from February 10-18.[289]

On February 16, Murphy received a promotion to 1st Lieutenant, and was assigned to division headquarters as liaison officer. Murphy is not pleased. Although he hates what is happening, he does not want to be granted special favors. He is concerned about the men he had been leading, so much so that when he learned that his old company had been pinned down at the Siegfried Line, he slipped off to check up on them, and led them to safety.[290] His own report in *To Hell and Back* was substantiated by his one of his men, Charles Owens, in an interview for the *Audie Murphy Research Foundation Newsletter*. Owens recalls, "And so Murphy says, 'Private Owen get your bazooka and let's go up there and hammer on that Siegfried Line.' ... [W]e had to fight our way through those zigzag trenches to get up to that first bunker. The main entrance to the bunker was around behind and down to the second level. And it had a big iron door on it. Murphy says, 'Private Owen, shoot that door with that bazooka.' So, I get up there in the hallway and shoot down at the head of the stairs. And there's a big old concussion. . . and smoke. [I]t blows me back. Murphy picks me up and says, 'Shoot it again. They're still in there.' And it just makes a little bright spot on the door. That door must have been tool steel or something. Shot it twice. And then all of a sudden, they start banging on the door. 'Comrade, Comrade!!!' They wanted to give up."[291]

    1st Lieutenant Murphy would return to Company B as its commander during the last days of the war in Germany, but for the most part, he saw no more front line action. The Army wanted to see that he went home alive. Keeping the nineteen-year-old Lt. Murphy away from the lines was not an easy task for his commanding officers, however. Fellow GI Gene Palumbo told the Audie Murphy Research Foundation of an incident that he witnessed one day in Germany. "we'd just got through a battle..., and I'm sitting down aside of the road.... I'm up on a little knoll looking down, and I think, 'What the hell?' There's four infantry guys and there's a guy in the middle there with four rifle guys around him. And I think, 'Jesus, that looks like Murphy. That looks like Murph!' And I yelled, 'Murph, what the hell did you do?'.... And he yells up at me, 'Ah, that goddamn captain's scared I'm gonna get myself killed. He won't let me stay up here." So I says, 'Well, good luck to you," and he says, 'Good luck to YOU.' And that was it."[292]

On leave, shortly before V-E Day, he would visit Carolyn Price. According to Harold Simpson, she would write afterwards to Perry Pitt, "I do wish he'd accept a discharge.... However, I'm sure he won't. He's dreadfully tired, but determined to see this thing through to the end -- his or the war's. His luck has been remarkable but he can't hold out much longer."[293]

7
The Granting of the Boon

With the Congressional Medal of Honor awarded for his action at Colmar, the little, initially rejected kid has become the most decorated soldier in America's history. Through his own merits, his warrior's skill and his determination to see as few of the men in his command die as is possible, he has attained the "treasure," and is granted the Ultimate Boon: the gift of life. Campbell describes this boon as an elixir, a magic drink that gives understanding: a gift from the gods. This elixir is the ultimate goal of the quest. Attaining it is the symbol of having survived the journey into darkness. The elixir may take the form of a treasure, or Truth, gained in the process of fighting and overcoming the dragon, ogre, or tyrant who ruled the darkness.[294]

His quest is complete. The dragon has been faced and conquered. He has become the apotheosis: "the exalted, or glorified example" of courage under fire. It was a symbol he had earned first from his fellow soldiers. As far back as Anzio, the name "Audie Murphy" was spreading throughout the 3rd Division.[295] The medals and honors he received from his superiors merely acknowledged what was already fact.

Eisenhower's naval aide, Henry Butcher, refers more than once to the importance of clearing the Colmar pocket, the last area of German resistance west of the Rhine River, referring to it as a "troublesome snag," and a "thorn in our sides."[296] On January 17, 1945, three days after Murph returned to the front, Butcher wrote, "General Ike now feels that every last commander, including his superiors, understand what he means when he says we must secure a direct line on which to station defensive forces if we are to permit the greatest concentration of our forthcoming offensives. He still plugs away on his belief, consistently held, that the German forces west of the Rhine must be substantially defeated.... He has directed General Devers to clean out the Colmar pocket and get a line on the Rhine south of the Siegfried Line."[297] The value Eisenhower placed on the 3rd Division's actions in carrying out this order are clearly shown in a memo he sent in March to Generals Bradley and Devers. He was concerned that the actions of the division had been neglected by the press back in the states. "The actions of the 3rd Division and the remainder of the 21st Corps in the Colmar pocket might have been more strongly portrayed to the people back home," he wrote, according to Butcher. Ike continued to say in his memo that while it was generally not a good idea to single out one unit over another, certain actions needed to be especially commended.[298] He would also agree that no one individual could be singly responsible for such a victory. Still, if Lt. Murphy had not climbed aboard that burning TD, the siege on Colmar would have been seriously delayed, perhaps even lost. Randolph Campbell, in his book, *Gone to Texas: A History of the Lone Star State*, says it was, "probably the greatest display of courage under fire of any single soldier in the entire war."[299] At any rate, his actions that day certainly earned him the title of "exalted example."

Lt. Murphy heard the news about V-E Day while he was on leave at the French Riviera. He was too numb and exhausted to take it in. He had been primed for battle and death for so long that he could not conceive a future. "Like a horror film run backwards," he wrote of that day, "images of the war flicker through my brain. The tank in the snow with smoldering bodies on top. The smell of burning flesh." He could not feel joy, or even relief, but, "...as though a fire had roared through this human house, leaving only the charred hull of something that was once green."[300] If anyone had told him that he was about to become the symbol of victory, the hero expected to enlighten his homeland with the message learned from his journey, he would have thought it ludicrous. He wrote in *To Hell and Back* of what war had taught him. "I believe in the force of a hand grenade, the power of artillery, the accuracy of a Garand. I believe in hitting before you get hit, and that dead men do not look noble," but even then, a more positive message was beginning to emerge, one that would consolidate later and which he would, indeed impart. "But I also believe in men like Brandon and Novak and Swope and Kerrigan; and all the men who stood up against the enemy, taking their beatings without whimpering and their triumphs without boasting. Men who went to hell and back to preserve what our country thinks is right and decent."[301] Earlier in the book, at Anzio, he had told Helen, the nurse, about these same men. "I laugh," he said, "when I remember the people I once thought were the great ones of this earth. I've learned who the great ones really are.... they bitch, they cuss; they foul up, but when the chips are down, they fight like men."[302]

In later years, when he was at the height of popularity in his post-war career, he would remember, "A group of soldiers are ordered to advance against heavy fire and they all have fear," he would write, "I never met anyone who hasn't tasted it. What you hate is the man who won't conquer his fear, and instead uses the lives of his buddies to shield his own. In the front lines, especially, the answer to, 'Am I my brother's keeper?' is an emphatic yes."[303]

As he roamed the streets that day in France, a glimmer of hope began to dawn. He concluded his book with the words, "I may be branded by war, but I will not be defeated by it.... I will learn to live again."[304]

Part III: THE RETURN
San Antonio to Farmersville

"Did i tell you that i have been awarded the DSC and the Silver Star and the Bronz Star, and i already had a Purple Heart and two oak leaf clusters, and now i'm back at Regt. Hdqrs, waiting for them to give me the CMH, so i can come home. Am also to receive the Legion of Merit pretty soon, since that is all the medals they have to offer i'll take it easy for a while..."
Audie Murphy
Letter to the Cawthorn's from Germany,
April 1, 1945

The dragon has been slain, but the trials of Lt. Murphy's journey are not over. It is now time for what Campbell refers to as "...the paradoxical, supremely difficult threshold-crossing of the hero's return from the mystic realm into the land of common day.... He has yet to confront society with his ego-shattering, life-redeeming elixir, and take the return blow of reasonable queries, hard resentment, and good people at a loss to comprehend."[305]

Learning to live again did not come easily to Audie Murphy. Still suffering from the shock of two years of combat, he was now to suffer the shock of coming home. Although he was aware of his fame within the Army, and of his commanders' wish to keep him alive for his return home, the full extent of his fame did not hit him until June 13, when his plane landed at Lackland Air Force Base in San Antonio.[306] At first, he seemed to think that the fanfare was meant primarily for the generals and high-ranking officers on the flight, and was shocked to learn that he was who they came to see. He later told a reporter, Jane Wilkie, "I had no idea I had won any more medals than any other guy. I didn't even know what I had got for what. I was too busy to think about it. I remember when I went back to Fort Sam after the war, the town had a big blow-out, with a parade and flags and banners and the whole works. I didn't know anything about it--I guess everybody figured somebody else had told me."[307]

But the "boon of life" granted to the hero, as Joseph Campbell writes in *Hero with a Thousand Faces*, is not granted to him alone. It is his duty, having survived, to share the gift, and the lessons he has learned during his journey, in order to effect "the renewing of the community, the nation, the planet, the ten thousand worlds."[308] In some ways, this is often the most difficult task the hero faces, for he has been living in a world that is very different from the day-to-day world of his community. As Campbell says, there is "a certain baffling inconsistency between the wisdom brought forth from the deep, and the prudence usually found to be effective in the light world," an "inconsistency" that can never be fully explained to the uninitiated. The hero's attempt to do so is often misunderstood. The hero senses this difficulty, and the temptation to refuse the obligation is strong, so strong that some refuse.[309] But the true hero will recognize his obligation, and do his best to relay the message he received during his journey.

Audie Leon Murphy had been recognizing his obligations and accepting their responsibilities since his early childhood. He had continued to do so during the war. He would do so now. There was nothing in his make-up that would allow him to shirk them, even when he wanted to. But that first day back in San Antonio, almost did him in. "Anyway," he told Wilkie, "I went up to my room and had dinner in my room, and hit the sack. And there was this crowd, and the general stood up and talked about how proud everybody ought to be of this native son of Texas. I hear he got all the way to the end, where he said, 'And now it gives me great pleasure to introduce you to Lieutenant Murphy!' And nothing happened. I was blocks away sound asleep. Boy, did I get chewed up for that!"[310] Before the young lieutenant had slipped away to his hotel room, he had been exposed to band music, cheers, a twenty-gun artillery salute, a parade, and a luncheon reception. He had been told that this was only the beginning, that the celebration would continue all the way to Dallas, and from there to Farmersville, where another such celebration would take place among his friends and family.[311] Probably more frightened than he had been since V-E Day, Murphy refused a plane ticket and rode from San Antonio to Dallas with two reporters, Lois Sager of the *Dallas Morning News*, and an AP reporter named William C. Barnard. Sager told that he was obviously uncomfortable, and reluctant to talk about his experiences, but Barnard reported that Murphy had waxed quite eloquently, "Bravery is just determination to do a job that you know has to be done. If you throw in discomforts and lack of sleep and anger, it is easier to be brave. Just wanting to be back in a country like this can make a man brave," but Sager said he simply told them quietly, "I just fought to stay alive, like anybody else, I guess."[312]

When Murphy arrived in Dallas, he learned that he was to ride atop a fire engine, with its sirens blaring, all the way to Farmersville. However, when the entourage stopped in McKinney to pick up the mayors of McKinney and Farmersville, the young lieutenant got into their car and rode the rest of the way with them.[313] Many years later he would talk to reporter Thomas B. Morgan about combat. One of the things he spoke about in that interview was the noise. "In combat, you see, your hearing gets so acute you can interpret any kind of noise. But now, there were all kinds of noises that I couldn't interpret."[314] Artillery salutes, crowds cheering, bands, fire engine sirens, and other loud and unfamiliar noises had been blasting his ears from the time he stepped off the plane at Lackland. It is no wonder that he preferred to ride in the relative quiet of the mayor's car.

At Farmersville, there were not only crowds and cheers; he learned that he was expected to make a speech. There was no opportunity to slip away to a hotel room. It had to be endured. Photos taken that day of Lt. Murphy sitting on the grandstand show his discomfort. It was a blistering hot day, and the program went on for hours. When it was finally time for him to speak, he said simply, "About the best way I can express my gratitude is not to say too much. I know you people don't want to stand in this hot sun any longer and just look at me. What I want to say is that you can be proud of your sons and husbands who fought over there. I have seen them all and I know they're doing a good job." Reporter Lois Sager would write, "Audie is the kind of fellow who won't say a thing about himself. He can't understand the fuss that's being made over him. And he said he'd rather have faced a machine gun than to have made that speech."[315]

Farmersville was not the only town that made the claim for being Audie Murphy's hometown. Greenville claimed the honor as well, and had planned a rival celebration to take place on the 27th of June. In actual fact, neither town was actually his "home town." The farm he was born on was nearer Kingston than Greenville, and Farmersville was simply his sister's home, and where he had listed his official address during the war. If any of the towns in Northeast Texas might be considered his home, it was Celeste, where he had gone to school, and where most of his boyhood friends lived. And the people of Celeste seemed to know him better, since they realized that he would not want a lot of fuss. Their paper wrote, "There will be no fanfare when Audie arrives, for the people of this town actually know the little freckled-faced boy whose name has become a synonym for courage, and they realize he is sincere in saying that he wants no hero's welcome. However, there will be many warm and heartfelt handclasps given to the youngster who was reared by the people of this community...."[316] Murphy did manage to get in a few quiet days in Celeste between the celebrations in Farmersville and Greenville, although he was called upon to spend much of that time in Dallas making public appearances and the speeches which he hated.

The Greenville celebration was even grander than the one in Farmersville. After another short speech there, a crowd of teenage girls seeking autographs accosted him. When he was finally able to get away from the crowd for a while, he visited an old friend, Eddie Ayers, in his home. When Ayers told him how proud he was, Murphy told him quietly, "Eddie, the real heroes are dead." Something in the way he said it made Ayers sixteen year-old-son, Kenneth, remember. Kenneth would later write to Harold Simpson that it "made an impression on me that still lasts, and no doubt will for the rest of my life."[317]

The public appearances and news reports continued throughout the rest of the summer. The comments made by reporters could be summed up in a statement that appeared in a Dallas paper, "Any reference made to his great courage is actually painful to him. He didn't like killing. He killed Germans to save Americans. A dead German to him meant one more live doughfoot. And he doesn't like being applauded for doing what he considered his simple duty.... a swell kid, absolutely modest, sincere and genuine and unaltered by terrible experiences."[318] The statement is accurate except for the final comment concerning his being "unaltered by terrible experiences," for the truth is that Audie Murphy had been terribly altered by the experience of war.

The Wound that Would Not Heal

In addition to has physical wounds, Murphy brought home a mental wound as well, and unlike the physical ones, which showed, were treated, and eventually healed, the mental wound of war would haunt him for the rest of his life. The effects started showing at least as early as this first trip home. Family and friends told Harold Simpson of instances where he would freeze, and seem for moments to be in a trance, and would afterwards tell of flashbacks to some event triggered by some simple, everyday occurrence. Like many East Texas country boys, Audie loved black-eyed peas. So, of course, shortly after he came home, Corinne cooked them for him, but as he was about to dish them onto his plate, the family remembers he froze, put the bowl down, and left the table. Later he told his brother-in-law that as he looked at the peas, he suddenly saw the head of a dead German whose brains had spilled onto the ground. He never wanted to eat black-eyed peas again. On another instance, he lunged behind a sofa when he heard a teapot whistle from the kitchen. And again, when he was out hunting, he slipped slightly on a mudded slope, and looked up to "see" a German soldier coming over the ridge. In addition to the flashbacks, there were nightmares. Both Corinne and has cousin Elizabeth Lingo of Dallas told Simpson of nights when he was afraid to sleep because of them, and would turn on all of the lights in the house to keep from falling asleep in order to avoid them.[319]

Murphy's symptoms were not unique among returning war veterans. They were called by various names: "traumatic war neurosis," "combat exhaustion," "operational fatigue," among others.[320] The Department of Veterans Affairs has studied the emotional and psychological effect of war on "normal, healthy individuals." They recognize war as a "life threatening experience that involves witnessing and engaging in terrifying and gruesome acts of violence."[321] These individuals generally, like Audie Murphy, go into battle to protect their country and way of life, fighting out of a sense of patriotic duty. But in action, they find that, "The trauma of war is a shocking confrontation with death, devastation, and violence," and the study insists that, "It is normal for human beings to react to war's psychic trauma with feelings of fear, anger, grief, and horror, as well as with emotional numbness and disbelief. Most war heroes don't feel brave or heroic at the time, but they do their duty, despite often feeling overwhelmed and horrified, in order to protect others."[322]

Judith Herman, in her book, *Trauma and Recovery* writes about the psychological effect of combat on soldiers. She traces the history of psychiatric and psychological studies of what has come to be called post-traumatic stress disorder, or PTSD.[323] She writes that during World War II, "psychiatric casualties could be predicted in direct proportion to the severity of combat exposure."[324] According to Paula Schnurr, "Whatever the label, it is clear that [investigators] were seeing a condition much like what we now recognize as PTSD. For example," she continues, "Kardiner and Spiegel described a chronic syndrome that included preoccupation with the traumatic stressor, nightmares, irritability, increased startle responsiveness, a tendency to angry outbursts, and general impairment of functioning."[325] But the work done during and immediately following that war was directed primarily toward those men who broke down in combat situations in order to get the men back into action as soon as possible. In the years immediately following the war, psychiatrists began to recognize the inevitability of mental disorders in combat soldiers, finding them to be as common as physical wounds.[326] Herman reports that, "the strongest protection was the degree of relatedness between the soldier, his immediate fighting unit, and their leader."[327] Heather Formaini writes that due to the prolonged strain of combat on the autonomic nervous system, physiological changes occur. War neurosis and post-traumatic stress disorder damage the nervous system, leaving sufferers in a state of trauma preparedness. It is as though they are always expecting another 'battle' and the adrenalin rushes keep them hyper-alert, just in case they need to make a dash for the hills to hide from the aggressors.[328] These are the primary signs of PTSD, according to the *DSM-IV: Diagnostic and Statistical Manual of Mental Disorders*, published by the American Psychiatric Association.[329] Herman points to a series of studies beginning in the years just after the war which indicate how "the psychological changes of post-traumatic stress disorder are both extensive and enduring… [Patients] do not have a normal 'baseline' level of alert but relaxed attention. Instead, they have an elevated baseline of arousal: their bodies are always on the alert for danger." Each incidence of the "repetitive stimuli" that would merely annoy most people, become, for the sufferers of major trauma, "a new, and dangerous, surprise," and the symptoms continue even while the individual is asleep.[330] The *DSM-IV* records that "symptoms may include difficulty falling asleep or staying asleep that may be due to recurrent nightmares during which the traumatic event is relived."[331] Even during normal daytime activities, "the human system of self-preservation seems to go on permanent alert, as if the danger might return at any moment."[332] The result of this hyper-vigilance is a "diminished responsiveness to the external world, referred to as 'psychic numbing' or 'emotional anesthesia' usually beginning shortly after the traumatic event."[333] Herman elaborates on this symptom, saying that, "The activities he participates in lack drama; their significance lies in what is missing.... Long after the event, many traumatized people feel as if a part of themselves has died."[334]

Herman also reports that these events have an affect on the individual's future relationships, that "traumatic events destroy the victim's fundamental assumptions about the safety of the world, the positive value of the self, and the meaningful order of creation."[335]

These people not only lose their concept of the world as a safe place, they lose the sense of being connected to others in any meaningful way. Sufferers of PTSD also carry a tremendous sense of guilt for having survived when their friends did not.[336] As Herman says, they "feel utterly abandoned, utterly alone, cast out of the human and divine systems of care and protection that sustain life." For the rest of their lives, she reports, many of these victims suffer from "a sense of alienation, of disconnection, [which] pervades almost every relationship, from the most intimate familial bonds to the most abstract affiliations of community and religion."[337] She adds that witnessing the death or intense suffering of others cause guilt feelings to be especially intense. "To be spared oneself, in the knowledge that others have met a worse fate, creates a severe burden of conscience. Survivors of disaster and war are haunted by images of the dying whom they could not rescue...." For the combat soldier, "witnessing the death of a buddy places the soldier at particularly high risk..."[338]

Again, these studies conducted during and immediately after the Second World War were primarily directed toward men who broke down in combat, and Audie Murphy did not. His symptoms did not appear until after the danger was over. During battle, he was able to fend off any feelings of panic and act rationally.

The answer to why Audie Murphy was able to withstand the traumas of combat during the war itself, but developed problems afterward might be seen in another study reported by Herman, dealing with a group of ten Vietnam veterans who were able to avoid the symptoms.

> These extraordinary men had consciously focused on preserving their calm, their judgement, clear connection with others, their moral values, their sense of meaning, even in the most chaotic battlefield conditions.
> They approached the war as a 'dangerous challenge to be met effectively while trying to stay alive,' rather than as opportunity to prove their manhood or a situation of helpless victimization. They struggled to construct some reasonable purpose...and to communicate this understanding.... They showed a high degree of

responsibility for the protection of others as well as themselves, avoiding unnecessary risks...challenging orders that they believed to be ill advised. They accepted fear in themselves and others, but strove to overcome it by preparing themselves for danger.... They also avoided giving in to rage, which they viewed as dangerous to survival...[339]

Her description of these ten men is almost identical to the picture of Audie Murphy as we know it, not only from *To Hell and Back*, but from the recollections of his fellow soldiers[340], *at least up to the point of Lattie Tipton's death*. The study underlines the impact that losing his closest friend had on him. The Department of Veterans Affairs reports that, "Many studies have shown that the more prolonged, extensive, and horrifying a soldier's or sailor's exposure to war trauma, the more likely it is that she or he will become emotionally worn down and exhausted," and continues by saying, "This happens to even the strongest and healthiest of individuals, and often it is precisely these soldiers who are the most psychologically disturbed by war because they endure so much of the trauma."[341] The events following Lattie's death, coming in quick succession, would have reinforced the traumatic effect. Shortly afterward, he shot at what he thought was the most terrible looking creature he had ever seen, only to learn that he was shooting at his own reflection in a mirror. He received a minor wound; he was not invulnerable. He won two Silver Stars for actions that he carried out alone. He accepted a commission only after the last of his original comrades was sent home. By his own account, he isolated himself as much as possible. He had lost the greatest protection the combat soldier has, the attachment to his group.

The *DSM-IV* indicates that, "there is some evidence that social supports, family history, [and] childhood experiences may influence the development of PTSD."[342] Herman refers to studies of stress disorder during and after the war in Vietnam which indicate that the adolescent soldiers were particularly at risk.[343] She states that "the younger, less well-educated soldiers sent to Vietnam were more likely to have few social supports on their return home and were consequently less likely to talk about their war experiences with friends or family. Not surprisingly, these men were at high risk.[344] Paula Schnurr concurs, writing, "parental discord, broken homes, and parental alcoholism were more likely with operational fatigue."[345] So Audie Murphy's youth and family background may also have been a factor in his delayed development of stress symptoms.

After the fourth of July, the pace lessened somewhat. Murphy requested and was granted an extension of his leave until mid-August. He took some time to rest, to hunt and fish, and to begin writing about his war experiences. Significantly, one of the first occurrences he put to paper was the death of Lattie Tipton.[346]

His fame went nationwide when *Life* magazine put his picture on its cover in July, and included an article covering the young hero's return to Texas. One result of this photo-article was a letter from James Cagney, inviting him to Hollywood. Cagney saw that the hero was exceptionally photogenic, and thought that he might have a future in motion pictures, and wanted to talk to him about it.[347] Cagney was only one of many people who wondered about what Murphy would do in the future. He was constantly asked about his plans. It was a difficult question for him to answer. Like most returning GI's, he had survived in part by blocking out the possibility of having a future. One of the standard jokes during the war was "What are your postwar plans?" Murph himself had employed it at Holtzwihr, shouting it over the field phone to the artillery commander after one of the blasts, when the commander asked if he was still alive. Future was a forgotten concept, and it took most of the returning soldiers some time to adjust to having one. Nearly everyone wanted to know what he would do now. The Army wanted him to stay in. His commanding officers in France wanted to get him into West Point, convinced from working with him that he could pass the entrance exam in spite of his lack of formal education. Businessmen who could see the advertising potential offered him positions with their companies. Local friends offered him jobs. Murphy knew his educational background would be a problem. He apparently considered staying in the Army, possibly going to West Point. He also thought of simply staying in long enough to learn a trade, perhaps in radio; he had worked in a radio repair shop before the war. He considered going to Texas A&M to study animal husbandry.[348] But Murphy was no more indecisive than any returning veteran. In fact, all things considered, he made his choices fairly quickly. Shortly after V-J Day, he received a letter from Col. Edson, his commander in Germany, encouraging him to try for West Point. Edson felt certain that Murphy's natural high intelligence would respond to tutoring, and that he would be able to pass the entrance exams. Murphy wrote back that his physical disabilities would prevent him from attending West Point. There is no record, however, that Murphy ever took a physical exam at West Point, so it is likely that he felt this to be the simplest way of saying that he would not be staying in the Army.[349] Before V-J Day, he had written an article for the *Dallas Times Herald*, stating that, "I don't know what I'll do [when my leave is up]. I have 146 points toward a discharge, but if the army has something for me to do that will help them, the army comes first. I won't be sent into combat again unless I request it. and I won't. I'm not a fighting man. From here on, I want to like everybody."[350] When his leave was up on August 18, he put in for a discharge and was given terminal leave until the papers could be processed.[351]

A few weeks later, on September 20, Murphy accepted Cagney's invitation and flew to Hollywood. As soon as Cagney met him at the plane, he realized what a toll the war and the publicity of the return had taken on the young man. Instead of putting him up in a hotel, as he had planned, Cagney took Murphy to his home, and had him stay in a guesthouse there, and gave him an opportunity for some badly needed seclusion. He discussed the possibility of a movie career with Murphy, during that first two-week visit, and wrote to him again after his return to Texas. By this time, Murphy had had time to think it over, and decided that a career in Hollywood was worth a try. He accepted Cagney's offer and returned to the guesthouse at the Cagney estate. He signed a contract with Cagney Productions and began to learn a new trade: acting.[352]

It had been a hectic three months for the young hero. He had accomplished the major goals he had envisioned when he thought about returning home. With gifts of War Bonds from a local promotional drive, he purchased a new house for Corinne and her family, and had his younger brothers and sisters taken from the orphanage to live with her.[353] The shock of fame was beginning to settle in. He realized that he had been made a symbol for all American GI's. Although he didn't want it, and was probably more frightened by that responsibility than he had been facing the enemy, he accepted the fact that it was what he was, and began to try to live with it. Like it or not, the country was looking to him, and he felt an obligation to try to live up to the image they held of him. It was as though he was not free to simply live his life by his own choices. He believed he owed a debt to the men who were left behind, and to whatever forces had seen to his survival. As he had all of his life, he accepted the burden of his status. He was already famous. There was nothing he could do about that. He needed an income quickly. He was still the main source of support for his brothers and sisters. Even with the new house, Corinne would need continued financial help. College would delay that steady income for at least four years. He did not have the time. And whether he was consciously aware of it or not, there was another factor, a mythological factor that made Hollywood a good idea. An actor has a tremendous opportunity to shape lives, as he knew from his own admiration for heroes from the movies he had seen in his childhood.

It was one way he could repay the debt he believed he owed his fallen comrades and the country that had honored him. Joseph Campbell writes that it is the responsibility of the returning hero to share the "boon of life," the "magic elixir," with the people of his community. But sharing that boon is an awesome responsibility, complicated by the fact that the people he is supposed to save often cannot understand the message he has to relate to them. The dark journey remains a mystery to those who have not taken it[354]

BOOK 2: DELIVERING THE MESSAGE
Introduction

If Audie Murphy's story were merely a Romantic adventure tale, it could be ended at this point. But myth and real life stories do not end when the adventure is done. Few truly mythological heroes simply ride off into the sunset. Their lives continue, and eventually, according to Richard Guches, they find they are "no longer in good graces with the gods," or with the community they saved.[355] The hero often returns to a world not ready to be reformed. He "encounters the resistance of the family," writes Jole Cappiello McCurdy, and, "to the hostilities one encounters when one wants to be different from the masses. Often the hero will be persecuted if she or he refuses to conform to collective standards."[356] In Joseph Campbell's words, "Martyrdom is for saints, but the common people have their institutions; the boon brought back from the transcendent deep becomes quickly rationalized into nonentity." He continues by asking, "How to teach again what has been correctly taught and incorrectly learned a hundred thousand times, throughout the milleniums of mankind's prudent folly? How communicate to people who insist on the exclusive evidence of their senses the message of the all-generating void?"[357] The same problem is encountered by the real life heroes, Audie Murphy included. Although they are often larger than life, they are human beings and the lives of human beings seldom have "happily ever after" endings. But even in myth, there is usually a period of grace between the adventure and the fall, and the end of the story, though often tragic, is always uplifting.

According to Guches, when the successful hero returns, he marries the princess, and becomes the new king.[358] Joseph Campbell recounts how the hero comes home to "bestow the magic elixir,"[359] and, no longer a warrior, becomes first a Lover,[360] and then an Emperor,[361] or as Carol Pearson refers to this phase, a Ruler.[362] It is during this period of his life, according to Campbell, that the hero becomes a Father, and if he is eventually unwilling to let go of the kingdom in favor of his sons, he becomes a Tyrant who must be overthrown by them.[363] Sometimes he turns the kingdom over willingly, and retreats from the world, becoming an Ascetic or Saint.[364] In other cases, though, according to Campbell, the hero becomes a redeemer, giving his life for the people he has ruled.[365] Pearson calls this phase of the hero's life the Martyr stage.[366] Saints, Redeemers, and Martyrs all understand that their own particular lives are not important in the overall scheme of the world, and sacrifice their fame and power for the good of the community.

The role of redeemer, or martyr, was understood by Audie Murphy even in his childhood. It carried him through the war, and would eventually determine his end, though that end would not come for some time. In the meantime, he would attain even more acclaim, and be recognized as a popular leader. He would marry, father two sons, and achieve wealth and recognition. But he would never be able to forget the dark journey. It would return to him at night in has dreams. He would live his entire life with its consequences. And, eventually, it would be the cause of his rejection by the very people he fought to save.

1
Stranger in a Strange Land

"My, oh, my! Ain't this a town?"
Audie Murphy as Yancey Hawkes in "The Wild and the Innocent"

Having come straight from the realities of combat, "with a game hip and a limp and with his nerves and whole temperament triggered for war,"[367] Hollywood and Audie Murphy did not immediately hit it off. The glittering facade struck him as garish and inauthentic. Richard Hubler reports that, "he escaped from the frying pan of public adulation in Texas and fell into the fire of Hollywood. He went to a succession of parties in the movie capitol which--since he neither drank nor smoked--bored him."[368] He was a serious young man who had seen too much of life's hardships. There was no place that he could fit in. "I had a choice of going to cocktail parties with the older set, or to ice-cream parties with the younger set,".[369] It may very well have been those cocktail parties that convinced Murphy he did not want to smoke or drink. And the "younger set," while nearer his own age, seemed too innocent and unworldly for him to have anything to say to them. "When you're young," he told a reporter, "war robs you of your perspective. The little things, like school days and parties and sports, that ordinarily would be so enjoyable and important to a kid don't mean much to a young soldier."[370] Kate Holliday reported in *Screenland* that, "He just cannot get excited about hot rods and juke boxes. He's seen a few other things. He also says that, both because of the war and his background, he can't remember ever feeling really young."[371] She also reported that Murphy was a totally unpretentious young man with a healthy sense of self-esteem: "…he's not the flamboyant kind of hero, not the kind who dashes into gunfire just to show off. Instead, he's almost shy, almost timid. What he does, and what he's done come, you decide, from another sort of courage, the kind that knows the unbalance of the odds and meets them anyway."[372] He would sometimes put himself down in public rather than appear self-centered. He did not like being in the spotlight, and did not think of himself as a hero. In fact, as Holliday continues, he told her, "I always want not to be a hero. Only a few people deserve that title--and I don't know any offhand."[373] But Murphy quickly found friends. Jimmy Cagney always had high praise for his young protege, and helped him get acquainted. Murphy was especially grateful to Cagney because he knew he had a lot to learn about acting. As he later told Richard Hubler, "[He] had no qualifications and no ambition for the job," but "couldn't afford to ignore it."[374]

Murphy's relationship with Cagney started off well. Initially, he took private lessons from Cagney himself. On March 7, 1946, he wrote home to the Cawthorns that he went, "almost everywhere with Jimmy and we have a lot of fun, I like him fine,"[375] adding that "I am fine and working every day. The work is easy, it consists mostly or reading and learning to speak lines correctly."[376] By summer of 1946, Cagney decided that Murphy was ready for more advanced instruction. He had Murphy enroll in the Actor's Labratory, where he received, "lessons in speech, voice, acting, singing, walking, and fencing."[377] He attended the Lab throughout the summer of 1946, writing twice during that time to the Cawthorn's that he was "very busy going to school"(June 28), and again on August 9, that. "I have been working awfully hard, going to school almost day and night."[378] Murphy left the Actor's Lab at the end of the summer, however; concerned with the groups extreme left-wing politics.[379]

Cagney had been particularly concerned about Murphy's Texas accent. His speech instructor at the Actor's Lab, Margaret McLean, commented that, "Audie's precious accent will be good to draw upon for character parts in the future, but is not standard speech for the stage and screen."[380]

Cagney also expressed concerns about Murphy's "hayshaker stride,"[381] which was probably due more to the slight limp which still remained from his wounds, since childhood friends in Texas had referred to his walk as being so graceful that "when he walked, he seemed to glide,"[382] and although fellow member of "B" Company, Albert Pyle, thought it "peculiar," he described more of a hunter's stance: "like someone slipping up on game."[383] The lessons in speech and movement were quickly successful, for the most part, particularly where his Texas accent was concerned, which he lost almost completely in his everyday speech, although he did, as McLean suggested, call on it in many movie roles. While he learned to walk without a limp, he developed a unique "gait" that would become a part of his trademark as an actor as the years went by.

Although Murphy would be grateful to Cagney for giving him his start in Hollywood (In 1949 the editor of the Farmersville Times would report that, "Murphy was high in his praise of Jimmy Cagney, who first introduced him."), his professional relationship with Cagney did not last long. Neither did Cagney's production company, which had developed out of salary disputes with Warner Brothers, and was too far ahead of its time to be very successful.[384] By the end of 1947, Murphy had performed in one movie, "Beyond Glory" with

Alan Ladd. "I had eight words to say," he told Hubler, "seven more than I could handle."[385] He got this role without Cagney's help. Since Cagney's company had nothing substantial to offer him, Cagney released him, realizing he could do better on his own.[386] Cagney's company folded shortly afterward.[387] It would be a year later before, as he told Hubler, "He got $750 for a day's work in a splendiferous picture called "Texas, Brooklyn, and Heaven,"[388]

Although he had begun to recover from the worst of the effects of combat, Holliday reports that, "He couldn't eat and he couldn't sleep Home was wherever he felt comfortable hanging up his field jacket. A noisy one-room apartment in Hollywood over a bus stop, or a motel in Dallas or a massage table in Terry Hunt's health club, on which he bunked for quite a while."[389] According to Holliday, Terry Hunt was, "the one man in Hollywood who gave him something more that pretty words." Hunt, who ran "Hollywood's best athletic establishment, ...not only loaned him a place to sleep, but slipped him a ten-spot or so when the going got rough."[390] Even during these rough times, though, the generosity he came to be known for was in evidence. Once, when his friend David "Spec" McClure was down to $1.80, Murphy split his last $100 with "Spec."[391]

In *Trauma and Recovery*, Judith Herman points out the three basic needs of an individual trying to recover from the effects of prolonged stress and trauma: safety, remembrance and mourning, and reconnection with other people.[392] These needs are recognized and worked with today, but in the period following WWII, the returning combat veteran was generally without help. Instinctively, Murphy set out to meet those needs as best he could. Today psychologists realize that the best source of safety comes from a supportive family system.[393] But in Murphy's family, it was the other way around. He had always been the provider of support, and was expected to continue doing so. His best means of giving them the financial help they needed was acting, which took him away from them, to Hollywood, a place where he felt, much the same as Heinlein's alien, like a "stranger in a strange land," where, as he told Hubler, "I have a nodding acquaintance with people I say nodding and they say nodding."[394] Maxine Arnold explains that, "He'd come to Hollywood at a time when the whole world, it seemed, wanted to forget war."

But Audie Murphy's personality was such that even in Hollywood he quickly found supporters like Terry Hunt. He also met and developed a lasting friendship with David "Spec" McClure, a journalist who worked for Hedda Hopper. Hopper herself became an avid

Murphy supporter. His quiet charm and lack of pretension found him several lifelong friends. But feeling "safe" was still difficult. At night, his dreams brought the life-threatening horror of war back into his world. He watched his friends die again on the battlefield, night after night. He saw the cross-hairs of enemy guns trained on them. He found he could stave off the worst of the anxiety that came with these effects of combat trauma by sleeping with a gun under his pillow, and keeping the lights on.[395]

Most people even then, and especially today, do not understand, but to a hunter, a gun is merely a tool. He uses it to provide food in much the same way a farmer uses a plow. To a soldier in battle, a gun means the difference between life and death. After the war, Murphy's damaged nervous system was always on the alert for new dangers, and he could stay calm, and avoid some of the symptoms, by keeping a gun close at hand. One of his most distressing dreams involved being surrounded by Germans while his gun fell apart.[396] In an earlier version of that dream, reported in *To Hell and Back*, he had only one shell in his gun, and he himself connected that dream to the situation of his childhood, where his survival depended on his ability to make that one shell count. Because of his hunting skill, that one shell had sufficed in the Texas backwoods, but during the war, in the "dark night" world of the battlefield, his skill alone could not keep him alive. After the war, the gun in his dreams fell apart because he knew that it was no longer of any real use. Murphy knew that he could kill. He also knew that in the world of society, the "daylight" world, he would not. He chose not to. Although he usually owned several guns, and sometimes carried one with him, he had a tremendous respect for the weapon's power. He was known to rebuke fellow actors, especially on the sets of his western movies, where guns were prevalent, when they "played" with them. Once, when co-star Hugh O'Brien challenged him to a "fast-draw" contest, Murphy agreed, but insisted they use live ammunition instead of blanks. O'Brien, not knowing Murphy well enough to understand his wry sense of humor, hurriedly backed off.[397] In fact, there were several people in Hollywood who did not understand Murphy, and tended to be afraid of him - not for who he actually was, but for who they perceived him to be, a situation that privately amused him, and one he quickly learned to use to his advantage.

He needed that advantage. Maxine Arnold, referring to him as "the lonely restless Joe you used to meet at a small cafe on Hollywood Boulevard for coffee and to exchange a few words about Texas," reports that, "Agreements made with him were broken again and again. Pictures promised him were never made. He'd got offers for advertising tie-ins and publicity package deals from those who wanted to cash in on his medals, but Audie wouldn't commercialize on his war record at all. He skimmed by on his $86 pension some of the time."[398] His friend "Spec" Mcclure would later write that Murphy, "would not play up to anybody who could help him in the film industry if he didn't respect them. Audie had a fierce pride, an innate dignity, a quick temper, and a devastating sense of realism with which he viewed the world."[399] Those qualities made him different from many people in Hollywood. People who made their livings through the illusion of film sometimes lost sight of the distinction between illusion and reality. Audie Murphy never did. Throughout his life, he maintained a reputation for integrity.

He also set out immediately to work on the second need of trauma recovery, remembrance and mourning. He had begun writing his memoirs almost immediately after his return.[400] He continued compiling stories of his experiences and especially those of his buddies who had died, and often talked of them. "Sometimes when he talked," reported Arnold, "the scars inside -- deep inside -- would bleed through. The gulf between soldier and civilian was just too painful to bridge." Consequently, Murphy wanted those lost friends to be remembered, not just by him, but by everyone.[401] By writing about and publishing his recollections, he could honor that loss. He had completed 353 pages in longhand when he met "Spec" McClure. "Spec" had been a member of the Signal Corps serving in Europe during the war, and had a basic grasp of the wartime situation. He served as a combination guide, mentor and secretary, prodding Murphy to finish the book. [402] Today, 50 years later, *To Hell and Back* still stands as the most intimate and immediate study of the individual in combat that has been written. It was not the story of Audie Murphy, war hero. It was the story of a group of GI's who struggled together and supported each other during one of the most difficult situations in our history.

Reliving the war was not easy. He spent many sleepless nights writing poetry, though little of it survives.[403] One exception is the poem attributed to Kerrigan in the book. The poem ends, "The crosses grow on Anzio/Where Hell is six feet deep."[404] Murphy's "remembrance and mourning" did not end with the book, as Arnold reports: "He was an officer in John Ford's chapter of "The Purple Hearts" and he visited veteran's hospitals to boost morale. "But this was almost too much for him, and he was understandably upset about the public's seeming apathy. "I just can't go into a hospital, it makes me too ill--seeing those guys lying there--stuck there like yesterday's newspapers, and so few people remembering them."[405]

The third need of recovery noted by Herman, reconnection, was also intuitively understood by Murphy. As early as June of '44, Murphy wrote home to the Cawthorn's that starting a family was going to be high on his priority list when he came home.[406] One of the favors bestowed on the returning hero is that of "Marriage to the Princess," and Murphy came home from the war ready to marry and start a family. His first romance, shortly after his arrival in Hollywood, was with actress Jean Peters. Their relationship was very intense, but as Shakespeare once wrote, "Too like the lightening, which ceases to be 'ere one can say, 'It Lightens.'" The relationship was already fizzling when Peters met millionaire Howard Hughes, whom she would later marry.[407] Shortly afterward, he met actress Wanda Hendrix. Their romance was picked up and spurred on by the press, who saw them as the perfect couple, and indeed, Murphy and Hendrix married as soon as he could afford to. But the marriage proved to be less than ideal. Hendrix, several years younger than Murphy, had trouble dealing with his nightmares, with the gun he still kept under his pillow at night, and with the moodiness and irritability which were also aftereffects of his combat trauma.[408] For Murphy's part, as he told a reporter in '51, "I thought I was going to have a housewife instead of a career girl. She was an awfully nice girl, but she wasn't ready for that." Characteristically, Murphy accepted the brunt of the blame for the failure of that marriage.[409]

"She had no more right around me than a lamb around a grizzly." he told Hubler, who reports that, "As it turned out, the union lasted exactly sixteen months. Audie ended up with two ulcers and the furniture; Wanda got a neurotic condition, low blood pressure, and the wedding presents."[410] Although the marriage did last 16 months, technically, they lived together only about three months. The Pollyanna press element, though, did not let go of their "storybook couple" lightly. Even at the time their divorce was being filed, and article appeared in *Motion Picture* stating that, "At present writing, the Murphy's seem to be plodding through the dark woods to the bright plain of marital happiness."[411] His second try at marriage was more successful. Murphy met flight attendant Pamela Archer shortly after his divorce was filed, and married her as soon as it was final. This marriage lasted. It gave him two sons, Terry Michael and James "Skipper" Shannon, both named after men Murphy considered his "surrogate" fathers.[412] In fatherhood, Murphy would find that sense of reconnection he needed. He was able to strike something of an "uneasy peace" with Hollywood.

2
The "Bad Boy" of Hollywood

A short time after Murphy's contract with Cagney was dropped, his Hollywood problems were compounded by family troubles back home in Texas.[413] And, as usual, Murphy was called in to solve them. Although he had bought a house for his sister Corinne, partly to enable her to make a home for his younger brothers and sisters who had been placed in an orphanage, the situation was not working. Corinne was having some difficulty looking after all six children: her own plus her youngest brothers and sisters. It was decided that Nadene and Joe Preston would have to move out. Murphy was able to arrange for his oldest brother to take Nadene, but Joe Preston was still a problem.

Fortunately, while he was in Dallas during the summer of 1945, he met a man named James "Skipper" Cherry, a Dallas theater owner. Cherry belonged to a group of theater owners who took an active part in Variety Clubs International. The club was "involved with the Variety Clubs International Boy's Ranch - a 4,800 acre ranch near Copperas Cove, Texas," according to an entry at the Audie L. Murphy Memorial Website. Through "Skipper" Cherry, Joe Preston was able to live there. The arrangement worked out quite well for Joe, and deepened the friendship between Murphy and Cherry. At one point, Murphy told Cherry he was considering leaving Hollywood since his career wasn't going anywhere. The revelation from Murphy happened to coincide with the early stages of a film production sponsored by the Variety Clubs, a movie called "Bad Boy," which would illustrate the work of the Boy's Ranch by telling the story of a troubled teen helped by the ranch. "Cherry called Texas theater executive Paul Short, who was producing the film, and suggested they consider giving Audie a significant role. Audie looked good in the screen test," according to the website entry, "but the president of Allied Artists did not want to cast someone with so little acting experience as a major character. However, by this time, Cherry, Short, and the other Texas theater owners had decided that Audie Murphy was going to play the lead or they weren't going to finance the film." Allied Artists went along. Murphy was cast in his first lead role.

"I'm really awful," he said of the role, "I rob somebody, I fight, I ride a horse to death. I do everything the Johnston Office will allow."[414] Murphy was nervous about the break. Lots of people were counting on him and had invested heavily in him. There was a lot riding on his success or failure. He knew his acting skills had not yet developed. He even joked during the filming about having "no talent."[415] But the movie was a success, and led to a picture with Universal-International, "The Kid from Texas," about another juvenile delinquent, Billy the Kid. The success of this movie led to a contract with Universal. His first movie under contract with U-I was less successful, however. "Sierra" had a story-line evidently aimed toward adolescent girls. He co-starred with his first wife, Wanda Hendrix. It was really her movie, a young girl's fantasy story where the heroine does the "questing" and saves the hero. Murphy's role served primarily as backdrop. Critics claimed the lack of success was due to Murphy's inability to handle romantic roles[416], but by the time the movie was released, the Murphy's had divorced. That knowledge didn't do a lot for the fantasy illusion, and contributed heavily to its box-office failure.

At any rate, U-I decided to stick with what had worked before, and put him in a string of "bad boy" roles.[417] He played Jesse James in "Kansas Raiders" and Bill Doolin in "The Cimarron Kid," and might likely have continued such roles were it not for a movie he made outside the studio. John Huston chose him to play "The Youth" in his adaptation of Stephen Crane's *The Red Badge of Courage*. Under Huston's tutelage, Murphy's latent talent came forward, and although that movie didn't succeed at the box office, it proved that Audie

Murphy could, indeed, act.[418] And over the years, Huston's film has gained stature. Today it is considered a classic. Although he attended acting classes at Universal for a couple of years, Murphy basically learned to act the way he learned everything else, including combat: by experience. He had little opportunity to learn acting in classes or by playing minor roles. After two bit parts, he stepped into lead roles immediately. He learned to act while starring in his first films.[419]

During this time he learned more than acting. He learned how Hollywood worked. Sometimes he learned the hard way, by recognizing his mistakes. He was "green" when he first arrived, and got into deals that created a heavy financial strain. He had agreed to make several movies with Paul Short, and had to buy him out when he joined U-I. He had bought the rights to Maureen Daly's novel *Seventeenth Summer*, thinking he and Wanda could film it together, but they divorced.[420] As he always had in the past, he turned these circumstances into learning experiences. Hollywood would have difficulty catching him off guard again. He quickly realized that in this world, he would have to watch his back as closely as what lay in front of him. It wasn't long before, as Maxine Arnold reported, "He'd stood off the German army almost singlehanded, but in life Audie was afraid to let his guard down lest when he wasn't looking somebody might slug him from behind."[421] "He was still living one hill at a time," she said, "And the way he drove an automobile didn't prove to lengthen it."[422]

Murphy could never bring himself to play the Hollywood game. He told a reporter in '51, "I'm not too impressed by Hollywood and it may be mutual. The studios think I'm difficult. They would come up with some screwy idea of me being photographed sipping a straw in a milkshake with some girl. It was silly and I balked at it.... I was naive and ignorant when I came to Hollywood," he continued, "I didn't know anything about contracts or the way they worked the angles."[423] Actually, even during these early years, there were quite a few people in Hollywood who were extremely impressed with Audie Murphy. Western director Budd Boetticher first met him at Terry Hunt's gym, where he was impressed by his pluck and courage in the gym's boxing ring even before he knew who he was. Eventually Boetticher pronounced him a "wonderful actor," commenting that he was "very good" even as early as "The Cimmaron Kid," which Boetticher directed.[424] John Huston, after working with Murphy in "The Red Badge of Courage," praised him for his onscreen charisma, and his "ability to win audiences."[425] Bill Mauldin, WWII cartoonist and Murphy's costar in "Red Badge," became a lifelong friend and admirer during the filming of that movie.[426]

Hedda Hopper went to bat for him with the studio executives who had opposed him as Huston's choice to play the lead in that same movie. As his stature in Hollywood rose, and his acting ability developed, more and more individuals there would praise his work, his attitude, and his intelligence.

Even though he had little opportunity for formal education, Murphy was, like the heroes of myth, born with extraordinary intelligence and insight. That insight had helped him to survive childhood and the war. Because of it, however; he tended to see not only war, but also Hollywood "as it really was." And he didn't always like Hollywood either.

3
Master of Two Worlds

"I have to admit, I love the damned Army. It was father, mother, brother to me for years. It made me somebody. Gave me self-respect."
Audie Murphy
from *Audie Murphy: American Soldier*

On June 25, 1950, five days after Murphy's 25th birthday, Soviet backed North Korean forces crossed the 38th Parallel and invaded South Korea. Two days later, for the first time in its history, The UN Security Council authorized military sanctions -- against North Korea. President Truman responded immediately, and American troops were sent to South Korea where they would form the bulk of a combined UN force under the command of General Douglas MacArthur. Slightly less than five years after V-J Day, American soldiers were again being sent into battle.[427]

Less than one month later, Audie Murphy entered the Texas National Guard. He was immediately promoted to Captain. That August, he would spend two weeks at what would be a series of summer camps, acting as a tactical instructor for new recruits. He told the press that if his country was going to war, he wanted to be prepared. Murphy and Wanda Hendrix had been granted a divorce that April, and although his career was picking up, he still was not happy in Hollywood. But he had contractual obligations to Universal Studios, so periodic Guard duty was the best he could do.[428] Then, shortly after his enlistment, he was offered the role of "The Youth" in "The Red Badge Of Courage," which began filming as soon as he returned from Ft. Hood. By the time filming was complete, UN forces in Korea had regained control of South Korea, and were rapidly pressing into the north. It seemed that the "police action" would soon be over.[429] During the filming of "Red Badge," Murphy met Pamela Archer, and the loneliness he had felt after his divorce came to a halt.[430] In late October, divisions of the Chinese Army entered the battle in Korea, and MacArthur ordered a massive offensive. The Chinese counterattacked, and by early January of '51, recaptured the South Korean capital of Seoul. The UN forces pushed back, and by April had re-attained their positions at the 38th Parallel. At this point, the action stalemated. General MacArthur, realizing that the war could not be won as long as North Korean troops were supplied from Manchuria, publicly advocated bombing Manchurian airbases. President Truman called him home and replaced him with General Matthew Ridgeway.[431] At about that same time, Murphy married Pamela Archer.

By the time he attended his second Summer Camp, they were expecting their first child. He continued attending Summer Camps in '52 and '53, and even, while attending the '53 camp, on July 17, signed up and was approved for Advanced Officer Training.[432] But on July 27 of that same summer, an armistice was finally agreed upon, and the troops were withdrawn.[433] Murphy bought a house in Van Nuys for his wife and young son and settled into his movie career.[434]

But Murphy could never be content with simply making movies. About the same time as the Korean "police action" ended, he began his involvement with another form of police action: a personal and life-long commitment to the war on drugs. In 1955 he appeared before a Senate Judiciary Subcommittee and told how he became involved. Two years earlier, he informed the committee, he had started accompanying the LAPD narcotics squad on several raids, originally to gain background information for a movie he was considering. But on one evening, he entered the house of a known user and found the man's children, three little girls under the age of five, playing in "dirt and debris" while their father sat in a stupor, his drug paraphernalia spread out in front of him, the girls' mother apparently "on the streets."[435]
The sight of those neglected children was too much for Murphy. His childhood background, having seen European children as helpless

victims of war, by this time, being a father himself, all contributed to his determination to fight for such children, as he told the committee, "in whatever way I can from this point forward, any time I get a chance." "I intend to do it," he said, and evidence indicates he kept his word.[436]

But the Army would continue to hold an active interest for Murphy for many years. He took steps to see to it that a military career was always an option. He did not attend Summer Camp in '54. He was busy filming a movie version of *To Hell and Back*, but in 1955, during a period that coincided with the pre-release publicity for that movie, he returned to active duty for two months, campaigning throughout the country for National Guard Recruitment. The next year he was promoted to Major.[437]

Murphy had been an adolescent when he entered the Army in 1942, and the military had played a major role in shaping his identity. Joseph Campbell tells how the hero is often pulled back toward the adventure of the dark journey, sometimes becoming, as he calls it, a "Master of Two Worlds," moving freely from one sphere, the everyday world, the world of "light," into the dark world of adventure. Having been through the dark journey, that world is often more comfortable for the hero than the world of common day, especially since those who have never taken the journey have a hard time understanding him, or of comprehending his message.[438] One reason it is difficult for most people to understand that message is the insistence most people have of seeing the world in sets of opposites, one part of which is always good, the other always evil. The archetypal concepts of "light" and "dark" fit this pattern. People connect "light" with purity and goodness, "dark," with badness and depravity. In an effort to see ourselves and our world as good, we repress all negative ideas and situations into the "darkness" of our unconscious minds, in the area Carl Jung refers to as the Shadow. Actually, the mythological concept of the hero's journey is a symbolic exploration of the darkness within each of us, and psychologically, *it is in that darkness where we find our greatest treasure.*[439]

An episode of the Star Trek television series of the mid-sixties had Captain Kirk split into two people, one totally evil, the other, totally good. What Kirk and the rest of the Enterprise crew learned was that people need the evil part of themselves as much as they need the good.[440] It is in that darkness that humanity finds the ability to assert and protect itself, its ability to take action and make decisions. Without these necessary attributes, people cannot take positive action. They become helpless victims of the uncontrolled aggression of others. One of the lessons that Murphy learned during the war was that there are positive values even in the greatest evil, and he came home to see that there was also great evil in what was purported to be the "world of light." "War brings out the very best in a man," he would say later. "You share everything, and you know that you can depend on the guy who stands shoulder to shoulder with you,"[441] and again, "War taught me how to get along with people, not to be selfish. War is a pretty good course in public relations."[442] Conversely, he pointed out that fear often brings out the worst.[443] Murphy clearly understood a psychological truth. War itself is evil, but warrioring is an essential part of being human.

Both the world we live in and the people who live in it are a complex mixture of the qualities we term "light" and "dark." The individual Audie Murphy is no exception. Harold Simpson points out that one of the best descriptions of Murphy came from Major William Wood, a CIA agent in Austin, Texas, during 1974, who had served with Murphy in the National Guard. He had attended several Summer Camps with Murphy, and continued to see him off and on afterwards. According to Simpson, Wood called Murphy a "person with three personalities...[one] a modest, humble, quiet, unassuming, never demanding or desiring recognition person...[second] a person of great generosity, with much compassion who had a genuine interest to share what he had with others." Then Wood continued his description of Murphy by saying that, "down beneath all of this was a third person, a real professional soldier, thorough and demanding of himself as of others. Give him a weapon, and Audie was a changed man --he was a tiger with a gun and a bayonet in his hands!"[444] This description of Murphy comes quite close to the description of one of Ireland's greatest warrior heroes, the mythical Cuchulainn. In Charles Squire's *Celtic Myth and Legend,* we learn that "[Cuchulainn] seemed generally small and insignificant, yet, when he was at his full strength, no one could look him in the face without blinking, while the heat of his constitution melted snow for thirty feet all round him."[445] The legend of Cuchulainn has many elements of the magic, as do most heroic tales, but the resemblance is still quite clear, and it accentuates the duality that is present in all heroes, indeed, in all humanity.

4
From "Duel" to "Destry"
The Camelot Years:
Retelling the Arthurian Legends on Screen

While serious critics often dismiss the movies Audie Murphy made during the early fifties as "formula" westerns, they served an important function. The Romance, whether set in the Middle Ages, the American west, or on the streets of modern Los Angeles, is a primary art form with its basis grounded in the same mythological cycle as the stories of Ancient Greece.[446] Jon Tuska, in *The American West in Film*, relates the basic plot of the legend of Perseus: "There is a helpless old king whose kingdom is menaced by a devouring sea monster. Each year an innocent victim is offered to the sea monster in propitiation until, finally, the choice has fallen on the king's beautiful daughter. At this juncture the hero, Perseus, comes on the scene, kills the sea monster, and thus rescues the princess. In due course he marries her and inherits the kingdom."[447] The story of the "Fisher King" is an old one, which has been retold many times and in many forms. Because the king is ill or wounded, his country lies desolate, often in the hands of a cruel ogre-tyrant who is usurping the weakened king's power until a brave young knight rides in, slays the usurper, and marries the king's daughter, becomes king, and restores health to the kingdom. Carol Pearson refers to this restoration as a "transformation," explaining that, "It rains, crops spring up, babies are born, and the people feel hopeful and alive once more."[448] The many adventures of the knights of King Arthur often tell the "Fisher King" legend in one form or another. The two knights most often connected to the story are the knights Percival and Gawain.[449] Originally, these two knights probably developed from the same character, whose adventures and quests often centered on the search for a "Grail." In the earliest stories, the "Grail" was a stone or bowl with magical powers, but during the later Middle Ages, Christian writers saw it to be the cup that Christ drank from, and made the quest a holy one. They felt the knight of the Grail stories to be a bit worldly for such a holy quest, and split the knight into two men: Percival (later Galahad), the Grail Knight, who was pure and innocent, and Gawain, a more worldly knight seeking adventure and treasure.[450]

European critics have always given more credence to the Western as art than have the Americans, recognizing the mythical quality of the genre. French critic Andre Bazin called it "the American film par excellence," referring to its forms as "signs or symbols of its profound reality, namely the myth."[451] British critic Jim

Kitses also upholds the Western as myth, pointing out that it contrasts the hunter's world of the wilderness with that of civilization: the individual pitted against society.[452] Rollo May calls the western, "our most powerful and compelling myth." He admits that "such is the power of myth," that when he took his own children to see western movies, "for their own pleasure and enjoyment--or so at least I told myself," that even knowing the outcome from having seen the plot countless times, "when the bugle blow[s] and the flag and galloping soldiers come over the hill, I am just as thrilled as I always was." He explains that, "the myth of the lonely cowboy was made to order for Hollywood and the American mood." He refers to an interview with Henry Kissinger by Oriani Fallaci, repeating that Kissinger, in explaining his own popularity with the American people said, "Americans like the cowboy who leads the wagon train by riding ahead alone into town." May concludes that "This early loneliness would seem to be connected, as a kind of cultural inheritance, with our lone ancestors, the hunters, the trappers, the frontiersmen, all of whom led a life of relative isolation"[453]

That same contrast of the lone warrior pitted against society is depicted in the Arthurian tales of the knight errant, knights like Percival and Gawain who would not accept society's answers and instead went alone into what was for each individual knight, "the deepest part of the forest."[454] Robert Foulke and Paul Smith show evidence that the Romance, as seen in those tales of Arthur's knights is a "primary narrative pattern," closely resembling legend and myth, which they "draw on." Foulke and Smith point out the relationship between those medieval tales and today's "movies, cartoons, comic strips, and television drama." They conclude that, "the popularity of these forms lies in the simplicity of the questions they raise and the inevitability of their answers." The questions arise, "in the suspense we feel over whether the cavalry will arrive on time, whether Dorothy will find the Wizard of Oz, whether Godzilla will be destroyed, and whether the Little Engine that Could, can. The romance pattern asks us to entertain these questions as if their were some doubt to the answer, which of course, there is not."[455]

    Rollo May is not the only individual to note the relationship between the western, the myth, and psychology. Richard Guches uses the western movie plot structure to explain Carl Jung's concepts of *persona, anima/animus,* and *shadow*. He explains how Jung used these terms to explain the three basic elements of the human personality, elements which draw heavily on the mythological "archetypes" in our "collective unconscious." The *persona* is the "actor's mask" we all use to face the world, or the person we want others to see us as being.

The <u>anima</u> or <u>animus</u> is the "life force," the part of us that keeps us alive and loving. (A man's anima has feminine characteristics, while a woman's animus is male. We tend, according to Jung, to fall in love with people who closely resemble our own contrasexual selves.) The *shadow* is Jung's term for the darker side of our personalities, the side we would prefer to keep hidden, often even from ourselves. Guches points out that these three elements in the "personal unconscious" of the human personality correspond to the hero, the heroine, and the villain, respectively, in western movies.[456]

Carol Pearson points out that, "the returning hero's task is always to bring life to a dying culture."[457] The Korean conflict brought home to Americans that World War Two had not put an end to the desolation of the first half of the Twentieth Century. The dragon had only moved to a different territory, and now, in the face of the mass technological power first unleashed on Nagasaki and Hiroshima, the best we could hope for was to hold it at bay. For hope, the country turned to its past, to the development of the west, and to the new young hero who had returned from the darkness of our "last just war," Audie Murphy.

In 1951, Murphy's growing popularity, coupled with his improving acting skills caused U-I to move him from the "bad boy" characters he had portrayed in his first films to a more genuine hero, a Western version of knights like Gawain and Percival. During the next few years, his popularity would grow to the point that in 1954, he would be voted the country's most popular western actor.[458] Critics invariably spoke of his credible performances.[459] His popularity developed in part because of the heroic roles he played, but primarily because of the "persona" he adopted to portray them. Although Murphy got a taste of "method acting" during his short stint at the Actor's Lab, the style he developed relied heavily on his growing ability to put himself in the position of the characters he played. His credibility on screen came from the personality that lay behind the mask: that of a quietly responsible, courageous, and capable young man determined to do the right thing at whatever cost to himself. Audie Murphy was the epitome of May's "lone cowboy," a perfect vehicle for the Hollywood western version of the "knight in shining armor."

In the first of these "Arthurian" westerns, *Duel at Silver Creek*, Murphy plays something of a transitional role. In the beginning, he is still a gun-slinging kid bound for trouble. When the Silver Kid rides into Silver City, though, he meets a sheriff with a crippled gun hand who convinces him to put his gun to a better use. He becomes the sheriff's deputy and helps him restore peace to the community by stopping a gang of claim jumpers. In the process he meets a young woman named "Dusty" Fargo, played by Susan Cabot, and falls in love with her. During the final scene of the movie, Murphy faces a new challenge for his acting career, as he romantically convinces Cabot's character to marry him. With her on-screen acceptance, he officially becomes a movie "hero."

The spark between Murphy and Cabot prompted U-I to put them together again in his next film, "Gunsmoke." In this movie, the "kid" has grown up. The plot, once again, is basically the same, but Murphy shows an added dimension in this film. Unlike many of the other "personality" stars, Murphy never played a character the same way twice. He had a knack of putting something unique into the "persona" even though the script's plot was often similar. There is a hint of deadliness and danger lurking under the surface of the soft-spoken Reb Kittredge. But Kittredge, in spite of his occupation of gunslinger, has a high moral character. When he realizes he has been brought to town by the evil town boss, Matt Telford, to kill an aging rancher who is holding out from selling his land, he refuses the job, and instead helps the rancher get his cattle to market in time to meet the deadline on his mortgage. The Murphy persona carries what Campbell calls the "Hero as Lover"[460] phase a bit further. Like Dusty Fargo, Cabot's Rita Saxon is a bit of a spitfire. Murphy does his best romantic work with such characters, women who are closer to equals in one way or another. In one scene, Murphy is shaving, shirtless, when someone knocks on the door. Naturally on guard, he pulls his gun before he opens the door to find Rita. When she suggests he put his gun away, he quips, "I sort of feel undressed without it," and she quips back, "You sort of look undressed even with it."[461] The scene has a quality much like that of Sir Gawain's encounters with the ladies he often met on his journeys.

This is the first movie where Murphy seems completely comfortable with "acting." He is in control of the character all through the film. He has changed his look to one he will carry throughout most of his westerns in the future. He wears a working cowhand's clothes and a sweat-brimmed hat. Director Nathan Juran was impressed with Murphy's professionalism, his "always knowing his lines" and "never making a mistake" as well as his ability to handle action scenes without requiring a double, according to Nick Clooney of American Movie Classics. Clooney also relates that Juran spoke of one scene in this movie in particular, where Murphy has to ride down a steep, slick hill and pull up directly in front of a close-up camera.[462] On screen, the action doesn't look that difficult until you slow the action down. When you do, much as slow motion and stop action can show an athlete's timing and skill, you see an image of masterful control and coordination between man and animal.

There are times in his next film, "Column South," (a movie that explored another facet of the Arthurian heroes, their honorable treatment of enemies, in this case, the Navajo) when Murphy seems less comfortable in his role. This film does not come off as well as the others he made during this time, probably because of the overly complicated script. But director Fred de Cordova, already well known as director of popular comedies like "Bedtime for Bonzo," and who later became best known as Johnny Carson's producer on *The Tonight Show*, was impressed, not only with his on screen talent, but with a situation that occured offscreen, on the movie set. Nick Clooney related that in his autobiography, *Here's Johnny*, de Cordova recalled an incident that occurred on the set of "Column South." As part of a publicity gimmick, General Mark Clark visited the movie set, only to be put down by Murphy for not remembering that even Generals salute Medal of Honor winners. When de Cordova asked Murphy why he did it, Murphy replied, "Too many men who didn't have to died at Anzio."[463] What de Cordova may not have been aware of was that Murphy had just returned from Summer Camp with the 36th Division. The 36th's memories of Clark were hardly pleasant.

In fact, shortly after the war ended, the division brought Clark up on charges that he had unnecessarily sacrificed the lives of many T-Patcher's at San Pietro.[464] The general was officially cleared of the charge, but his reputation for putting his own publicity ahead of the safety of his troops had lingered. It may be that Murphy behaved so uncharacteristically because he thought that the incident might give tacit approval to Clark's actions, and resented being used. [465] In the end, although the movie got poor reviews, Murphy was exonerated. According to Gossett, the critics agreed he was the "most believable member of the cast."[466]

In his next two outings, Murphy played characters closer to the knight, Percival: a naïve, innocent youth questing for truth. In "Tumbleweed," he plays a drifter who, after signing on as guide for a wagon train, is falsely accused of cowardice and desertion, and sets out across the desert to prove his innocence. This movie carries all the aspects of the hero's adventure as explained earlier. The hero is aided by several helpers, including a "friendly animal with magical powers," the horse, Tumbleweed. The reader may recall that the "dark Journey" is frequently symbolized as a "desert wasteland," and that the hero often finds a "magic elixir" which restores life to the community.[467] Jim Harvey, the hero of the movie, finds, with the help of the horse, Tumbleweed, a hidden spring which keeps the posse that is chasing him from dying of thirst. The Percival-type hero, because of his naivete, often stumbles onto the truth, as does Jim Harvey in "Tumbleweed," and as will Clay O'Mara, the hero of Murphy's next film, "Ride Clear of Diablo."

Clay O'Mara is a railroad surveyor who learns that rustlers have murdered his father and younger brother. When he realizes that the mystery has not been solved, he returns home to settle the question himself. He is aided by an intriguing "helper," an outlaw named Whitey Kincaid, ably played by Dan Duryea.[468] Naively believing that the sheriff and his father's lawyer, as representatives of the law, could not possibly be guilty, he refuses to listen to Whitey. He continually puts himself in danger before Whitey finally forces him to see the truth: it was the sheriff and the attorney who committed the murder. Murphy's skill as an actor continues to improve. "Ride Clear of Diablo" is the first movie where Murphy is placed in a situation where he must play off an actor of Duryea's stature. The interplay between them, which runs through the movie, is very effective.

"Drums across the River" is the third movie of this period to explore the plight of the Native American. (In "Column South," a devious general is using the Navajo to speed up the onset of the Civil War. In "Tumbleweed," the Yaqui are duped into attacking a wagon train by a greedy miner.) Gary Brannon, the Hero of "Drums" hates the Utes because one of them killed his mother, until he is forced to spend some time with the tribe and comes to know them as honorable people. In one way or another, each of these movies explores the Arthurian concept of the noble enemy. War and aggression are understood in this concept as a necessary part of life. The enemy is not a despised savage, but a worthy opponent involved in a struggle of equals. Today we realize that the situation faced by the Native American cultures was not so much a struggle of equals as it was an attempted extermination of a non-technological people by a marauding force with too much man- and firepower for them to withstand. Still, at least in these films they were not portrayed as brutal savages, and the real villains were the greedy white men who wanted their land. Murphy's mother was said to have been part Native American, and his wife, Pam, is part Cherokee.[469] It is not surprising that he never participated in a Western that did not treat these cultures with respect. In the one instance where he played a character who did not, that character was clearly in the wrong, and his purpose in playing the character was obviously to show by negative example the evil of racism. That character will be explored in detail in a later chapter.

Max Brand's novel, *Destry Rides Again*, was the basis for three movies and a stage play.

The version generally credited with being the best was the '39 version starring Jimmy Stewart and Marlene Dietrich. Much of the credit for it's rating goes to Dietrich. The '54 version, starring Audie Murphy and Mari Blanchard at least runs a close second.[470] Murphy does more that hold his own against Stewart. He puts his own stamp on the character, and as Gossett reports, was said by one critic to have come closer the Brand's original character than any other actor.[471] Once again, Murphy is called upon to add a new dimension to his acting talent. "Destry" is a comedy, and Murphy demonstrates his ability to bring his quiet, somewhat intellectual sense of humor to the screen. More important from a mythological point of view, in this role, unlike the previous movies from this period, where he played out the hero's adventure, Murphy now portrays the hero of "The Return," a man who has finished his wanderings, has found the answers, and delivers them to the community. Much to the embarrassment of the sheriff who has hired him as deputy, he does not wear a gun. He "doesn't believe in guns," he says.[472] Peace can be maintained by the use of law rather than violence. The townspeople soon learn that his pacifism is a matter of choice, that he is perfectly capable of using guns if necessary, and in the course of the movie, it does become necessary. But once peace is restored, the guns are put away again. The message is clear.

Violence is a bad solution to problems, and should only be used as a last resort. Our hero has come full circle. From his early days as a "bad boy" he has matured into a thoughtful leader of men, a "keeper of the law."

The audience reception of this Murphy "persona" is overwhelming. He is now not only the country's favorite Western star; he is considered one of the two top rising stars of any genre.[473] His physical stature has increased as well. Oddly, the same Hollywood system that kept it a secret that Alan Ladd was only 5'6" did not go to any great lengths to enlighten the public that Audie Murphy was growing taller. In 1967, when Thomas B. Morgan visited the Murphy home for an interview, he was surprised to see that Murphy was of average height, "about 5'10"." Murphy explained to Morgan that he had continued growing after the war, during his early twenties. "Wouldn't you know," he joked. "It was that dern helmet holding me down all the time."[474] He continued to impress the producers and directors of his movies for his talent and professionalism, developing a reputation as a "one take" actor who understood the limitations of time and budget and did not insist on reshooting a scene over and over. He made several additional friends among his co-stars: Jack Elam and Denver Pyle still remember Murphy as a valuable friend as well as a fine and a professional actor.[475] Universal Studios decided to make a major move with their star. His next film will be a reenactment of his autobiography, *To Hell and Back*, and he will play himself.

5
Reliving Hell

Audie Murphy did not make the decision to film his war exploits lightly. As early as 1953, he told Richard Hubler that Universal wanted to make the film, and he had his reservations. "It was a lousy book," he told Hubler, "because it was a lousy war."[476] Universal seemed intent on making the war seem a little less "lousy." As Sue Gossett reports in *The Films and Career of Audie Murphy*, "The book strove for realism, and the movie, for idealism."[477] Murphy's reasons for accepting this change may have been political. Murphy would likely agree with the statement that war is always evil. At the same time, he would be aware that in this world, we do not always have a clear choice between good and evil. Sometimes we are confronted with two evils, and our responsibility becomes that of making the choice as to which of the two is the lesser. Like Tom Destry, Audie Murphy was aware that in an imperfect world, aggression is sometimes necessary to stop aggression, and that our Army is a vital part of our maintenance of peace. He was concerned about the apathy of the American people towards the servicemen during the Korean conflict, which indicated that many Americans were so opposed to the risk of war that they were turning their backs on the country's warriors. It seemed an appropriate time to remind the public that there was such a thing as honorable war, and that in any case, the men who sacrificed their own lives and safety to defend the rest of us needed to be honored. The movie, "To Hell and Back," was designed to do that, so the emphasis was naturally different.

When the studio decided that it would be logical for Murphy to play himself in the movie, he balked. His life had finally begun to reach a degree of stability. Reliving the war a third time would be difficult, he knew. He was also concerned about his ability to play himself. He told *Los Angeles Times* reporter John L. Scott, "I didn't want to do the picture at all at first because I couldn't possibly analyze my own character like I could a fictional one."[478] He finally decided that it was more important, at the time, to see to it that America's soldiers were honored, and agreed to play himself.[479] There were several "perks." He would have an active hand in the production, scripts, and casting. And he would be paid substantially more than he had on other productions, not only in salary, but in a percentage of the profits.[480] One of the major contributions Murphy made to the casting of the movie was to choose his fellow actor and friend Charles Drake to play the role of Brandon, the fictionalized version of his close friend, Lattie Tipton. Drake and

Murphy had already co-starred in "Gunsmoke," and their off and on screen mutual admiration would prove an invaluable asset to this production as it would be to several movies they would make together in the future.

Once production started, he realized it was going to be even more difficult than he thought. First, there was the problem of relating, not only the war experiences, but also the suffering of his childhood to the scriptwriter and director. And as filming began, he found that actually reliving his experiences in front of the camera was painful, "It was the smell," he told a Screen Album reporter, "It brings things back so sharply."[481] One of the more difficult things he had to do, he learned, was to give the same orders he had given during the actual war. He found himself wanting, "to save one guy's life in battle, maybe, by telling him to go one direction instead of another," he told a reporter for the *Dallas Times Herald*.[482] Sometimes, in battle scenes, Gossett tells us, he would forget it wasn't the real thing, and would continue the action even after director Jesse Hibbs yelled, "Cut!"[483] Not everything about making the film was unpleasant. Murphy was an active father, always involved in the life of his two sons. His oldest son, Terry, had a small part in the movie, playing Murphy's youngest brother, Joe Preston, as a small child. Terry's ad-libs often kept the whole company in stitches, and once, during the filming of a battle scene, Terry, watching from the sidelines, stopped the action by yelling, "Look out, Dad!"[484] Murphy also managed to joke about some of the technical problems, as when the machine gun on the tank destroyer jammed, and the scene had to be stopped while it was repaired. He laughed to director Jesse Hibbs, "If this had happened during the real thing, we wouldn't have to bother making the picture at all."[485]

Still, he was concerned that the movie portrayed him as more of a hero than he believed himself to be. He told John L. Scott that he was "a lot braver in the picture." explaining that "Bravery under fire sometimes happens because a soldier, particularly an infantryman, is actually safer lying flat on his belly firing his rifle than running away."[486] Harold Simpson reported that, "Acting in the film also brought back the agonizing nightmares...more terrible than usual."[487] Eventually, the movie was completed and premiered in San Antonio, Texas on August 17, 1955.[488] It was a phenomenal success, both financially and critically.[489] Afterward, he told a reporter, "I was very glad when the last scene was shot...because living through the war three times [was] just too much.... World War II is really over as far as I am concerned. I don't want to go through it again -- ever."[490]

6
Fatherhood
The Hero as Emperor and/or Tyrant

When the returning hero lays aside his sword and takes a bride, Campbell tells us, he also takes up the "scepter of dominion, or the book of the law."[491] He becomes what Campbell refers to as Emperor, what Carol Pearson calls the Ruler[492], and what Richard Guches labels the King[493]. His primary role moves from that of action hero to father.

Throughout the 1950's Audie Murphy was consistently listed among the top 10 most popular stars in Hollywood.[494] By 1957, Audie Murphy owned, not only a house, but a yacht, a ranch, and a private plane.[495] Actually, he owned several ranches. Most of them were investments, bought and sold quickly for a substantial profit, but his ranch in Perris, California was a working ranch. In addition to his movie career, he bought, sold, and bred both thoroughbreds and quarter horses, many of which were champions. These material possessions though, were not nearly as important to him as a less tangible award given to him at that time. He was chosen "Picture Pop of the Year" by the Midwestern Fan Club Association.[496] The former Warrior is now both Emperor and Father. And Audie Murphy took more pride in fatherhood than in any of his possessions or accomplishments.

The hero in myth cannot stay young and heroic forever. This is true of real-life heroes as well. The transition from the youth, the young hero in action begins with his atonement with his own father, with the realization that "I and the father are one" and continues after his marriage to the princess and actually becoming a father himself. Once the hero has sons of his own he must prepare to step down, to one day turn over the role of leadership to those sons. If he cannot, he becomes a tyrant, and it will be up to those sons to conquer him.[497] This transition is easier for the hero who has come to terms with his own father, a difficult task in the case of Audie Murphy who had more than enough reason to hate his own natural father. Earlier in this book it was reported that in France, Sgt. Murphy had seen his own reflection in a mirror and shot at it, thinking it an evil enemy. It has been explained that mythologically all enemies are the father, and for the warrior to get beyond that role, he must come to the realization that "I and the father are one." This acceptance eventually leads to "atonement" with the ideal Father archetype, even when the personal father is a negative force. Through this "atonement," Murphy was able to understand the role a positive father played, was able to see beyond the abusive, neglecting image he saw in his father, and become a loving father to his own sons.

Becoming a father was an important milestone in Murphy's life, and allowed him the reconnection that is so important in trauma recovery. His relationship with his own sons, Terry and "Skipper" was a vital one. It is significant that they were named for two men who served as positive father figures for Murphy when he first returned from the war, Terry Hunt and James "Skipper" Cherry.[498] Murphy took an active role as father, not only as the family breadwinner, but also as nurturer and caretaker. In 1955, Murphy gave an interview to reporter Maxine Arnold. The result was an article called "The Personal War of Audie Murphy." In that article Arnold relates the obvious commitment Murphy had to fatherhood. During the interview, which took place at the Murphy home during a respite from the filming of the boxing movie, "World in My Corner," the father would occasionally be distracted to deal with his two young sons, gently stopping three-year-old Terry, for instance, from strangling little "Skipper" with a lasso. (He took care of the boys himself that day, but called on his wife Pam to take care of the dog when it appeared in the room with a suspicious piece of cloth between its teeth. "Ranger's got my gloves again," Arnold reports him as saying "mildly," "--or else he's grabbed the gardener.") He did not indicate to Arnold that active fatherhood was a particularly easy job. "I come to the studio and work out three hours in the boxing ring and I'm not too tired," he told her, "I stay at home with these boys three hours and I need a vacation." Then he elaborated on plans he had to build a mock-up jet plane in the back yard for Terry because, "[He's] deserted the Infantry. He's a jet pilot now." He explained the importance of the project by saying, "The boy's so mechanical-minded I want him to stay interested."[499] Through his inward knowledge of the "Father" archetype, Murphy, well aware of his own father's deficiencies, was able to give Terry and "Skipper" what he never had. One of the valuable gifts he gave his sons was his time. Publicity photos throughout the fifties show him taking the boys with him to the Universal lot. Current child psychology emphasizes the importance of the father-son relationship in a society where young boys see little of their fathers and know nothing of a father's work, since it usually takes him away from home.[500] During the last few years the "new" concept of fathers taking their sons to work with them occasionally has gained much interest. Audie Murphy was doing it forty years ago. The boys also spent a lot of time with their father at the Perris ranch, which he called AM Farms. A photo-article, "Rancher Audie Murphy," showed pictures of Murphy and the boys at the ranch which included, in addition to the horses, several dogs, and a pet chimpanzee.[501] Murphy once referred to children and animals as "the only all good creatures left."[502] Heather Formaini writes that, "fathering puts a man in touch with himself, and brings into being a heart which men sometimes feel they do not have. It connects men to the vulnerability and fragility of children and thereby to their own feelings of vulnerability and fragility. *It opens up the humanity which may have been cast into their own shadow personalities at the time of dis-identification with the mother.*"[503]

In later years, as the boys grew older, out of respect for their privacy, he did not allow publicity pictures to be taken of them, but he continued to spend time with them whenever he could. Thomas Morgan relates in "The War Hero" that Murphy was planning some time for the three of them to be together before he left for Algeria in '67.[504] By that time, he was aware that they were growing up and needed to be free to make their own choices. He did not expect them to follow in his footsteps. In fact, he hoped they would not. Murphy was always embarrassed by his fame. He did not seek recognition or wealth. He preferred the company of "ordinary" people to the rich and famous, a simple life to the typically glamorous life of Hollywood stars. And he lived his life as he believed life should be lived, giving his sons himself as an example to follow.

Campbell tells us that many heroes have trouble stepping down when the time comes to turn the "kingdom" over to their children.

Heroes who do not become tyrants must then be overthrown by their own children if the kingdom is to flourish.[505] These tyrants never come to terms with the "face in the mirror," according to Campbell. Instead, they insist to themselves that they are different, better than other people. In order to hold on to this illusion, they have an intense need to control other people, especially their own children.[506] Murphy did not live to see his sons past young adulthood, but he had already begun to turn the spotlight over to them: They both had roles in his last movie, "A Time for Dying," a movie which he produced.[507] One role Audie Murphy would never play was that of the ogre-tyrant.

7
The Freedom to Live

"The battlefield,' says Joseph Campbell, "is symbolic of the field of life, where every creature lives on the death of another."[508] This is the heart-sickening realization that each hero comes face to face with during the dark journey, when he confronts his own evil and realizes that he is no different from the enemy he fights. Campbell relates the story of the Hindu hero, Arjuna, who when seeing many of his friends in the enemy ranks, comes to the realization that the only purpose for war is greed, and decides that it would be better to die on the battlefield than to survive and live with his guilt. (This "heart-sickness of battle"[509] has been noticed by Homer and Shakespeare as well, and what we now call PTSD, during the American Civil War, was known as "soldier's heart."[510]) But Vishnu appears to Arjuna, and points out that his death will not change the outcome of the battle, that it is impossible for man to understand the ways of God, much less affect the outcome of situations that have already been decided. The hero who comes to terms with this reality no longer has any need for the attachments the rest of the world finds so important. He understands that power and control are illusions, that we are imperfect beings living in an imperfect world. The hero becomes an instrument, or as Campbell says, a "vehicle of the terrible, wonderful Law, whether his work be that of butcher, jockey, or king."[511] Having delivered his message, he accepts the "freedom to live," not expecting any favors for his sacrifices.

After completing the movie version of "To Hell and Back," Murphy attempted to focus on just living. At home, he spent as much time as possible with his sons; he maintained close contact with a growing circle of friends which included several fellow actors as well as individuals in other lines of work, but still refrained from entertaining simply for the sake of his career; he applied much of his new wealth toward helping others, not as a philanthropist, seeking recognition, but quietly, simply as a friend. For the next few years he would concentrate on his acting career. He negotiated a new contract with Universal that would give him more freedom to make pictures on his own, and more choice in the scripts within the studio.[512] He stopped playing the "brave knight," although he always preferred working in the Western genre. During these years he would portray a boxer, a preacher, and an army deserter. He would move out of the Western format, do farcical comedy, play villains, smugglers, bastards, and bigots. His acting talent flourished, and the critics started to agree with the general public, that this was an actor to be contended with. He continued, for the most part, to develop the same basic style of acting that had established his popularity during the early fifties, drawing comments from reviewers concerning his "sound," "sensitive," and "convincing" portrayals.[513]

In his first movie after "To Hell and Back," "World in my Corner," he played a boxer, a New York street kid who, not unlike Murphy himself, fought his way out of poverty. He threw himself into the role, working out three hours a day, sparring with actual welterweight fighters, several of whom played his opponents in the movie.[514] His efforts paid off in the reality of the boxing scenes on screen. Gossett reports that, "Los Angeles boxing experts, invited to the studio were amazed at the rugged nature of the cinematic warfare. Never before had they seen two 'actors' exchange such solid blows for the sake of movie cameras." She also reports that director Jesse Hibbs said, "he was determined to look like an expert in the ring, no matter how many hard punches he had to take to deliver one." There are dramatic scenes in the movie as well, where Murphy is outstanding. In one, he takes co-star Barbara Rush back to the slum where he was born, and talks to her about, "what [living there] does to you. Makes you just fight to stay alive, all the time wondering if it's worth it. I'm never coming back to the nothing that is here," he tells her bitterly, "even if I have to beat everybody's brains in - crowd the whole world in my corner and belt it right on the chin."[515]

His next role was based on the true story of John Phillip Clum, Dutch Reformed ministerial student turned Indian agent, in "Walk the Proud Land," which Tony Thomas includes in his book, *The Best of Universal.*[516] *In The Films and Career of Audie Murphy*, Sue Gossett points out the high praise given to Murphy by the critics, one of whom said, "Audie Murphy proves himself a first-rate actor capable of handling a role fraught with difficulties and potential pitfalls."[517] In an interview for *Screen Stories*, he talked seriously about himself as an actor for the first time. "I always play Audie Murphy," he told the reporter, "Of course I read up on the character I'm playing and analyze in one way or another how he thought as well as acted. But when I say something in front of the camera, I say it the way I mean it." His statement was backed up by director Jesse Hibbs, who added, "Audie always thinks about what he is doing. When the actor does that the action in front of the camera is smooth and honest. The camera is able to read Audie's thoughts through his eyes."[518]

After filming "Walk the Proud Land," he tried a venture of his own. He co-produced and starred in "Guns of Fort Petticoat," a tongue-in-cheek story of an Army deserter who trains a group of women to fight the Comanche. Murphy's character deserted because he could not condone Chivington's massacre of the Cheyenne at Sand Creek. He returned to his home in Texas knowing that the Comanche would retaliate, and that the men were all fighting in the Civil War. He has double trouble in this role because the women think of him as a traitor for having joined the Union Army instead of the Confederate. Gossett relates how Murphy, in order to make the scenes realistic, "trained the 40 women in the cast how to handle guns under military discipline.... For a week before the camera rolled," she writes, "Audie presided over a stiff training regimen in the Arizona location. It involved a 5:30 a. m. rising, roll call, calisthenics, close order drill, hikes (short ones) and then target practice with rifles."[519] Jon Tuska refers to this movie in his book, *The American West in Film*, referring to the way that Western heroines often come around to the "masculine" idea that guns and violence are sometimes necessary.[520] Although the movie was hardly "G. I. Jane," it was unusual for the time period in that it made the point that women could fight as capably as men when fighting was necessary.

"Joe Butterfly," Murphy's first and only farce, was more popular in Japan, where it was filmed, than it was in the United States.[521] The critics were less pleased with this role. There are times in this movie when he does not seem quite comfortable, probably because of the difficulty of looking within himself to find the source for a character who was as totally irresponsible as Johnny Woodley, the *Yank* magazine reporter frolicking around Tokyo during the first days of the occupation of Japan. Even in this movie he has his moments, especially when he is trying to convince George Nader, his costar, that the hatred must end - that they must come to know the Japanese as people, and put the war behind them. The movie, and Murphy's performance has stood the test of time, however. Recently on a segment of American Movie Classics's "Matinee Classics." Nick Clooney referred to Murphy's portrayal as "remarkable and offbeat."[522]

His next film, "Night Passage," fared better with the critics.[523] In this movie he plays a villain for the first time since his "bad boy" days. Jimmy Stewart plays the "good guy" in this movie. According to Sue Gossett, one critic said that, "stacked up against the seasoned [Stewart], Audie reveals a sheer talent for acting. He holds his own against Stewart throughout the picture."[524] The movie did well at the box office, but it was not quite the blockbuster the studio thought it would be. Part of the reason for that is that Anthony Mann, who was supposed to direct the film, backed out at the last minute because he didn't like the script[525], and there <u>are</u> problems with the script. Murphy and Stewart play two brothers, one "light" and one "dark." In the final scene, the "dark" brother, played by Murphy, dies after taking a bullet for his "good" brother. Herein lies the problem. This ending is somehow not psychologically satisfying. Jung, in his study of archetypes relates that we should not try to repress, or "kill off," the Shadow side of our personalities, but that we should recognize it as a vital part of who we are, and integrate it.[526] The tendency to block out the aggressive side of our natures was, at that time becoming a national trend, and showed in the movies coming out of Hollywood. We are still trying to overcome the result of this suppression.

Campbell points out that we can learn much from a particular society, not only by what it includes in its myth, but by what it leaves out. When a major part of the hero's story is omitted, we can be sure that something is being repressed.[527] One of the problems of the American Western, especially as it appeared during the early Fifties, was its insistence on the "happily ever after" ending. As a people, we rejected the possibility of the hero's fall at the same time we repressed the dark side of ourselves. Perhaps we had seen the awesome power of our own military technology, and did not want to face a future with that power in it.

But "Night Passage" is still a good film, primarily because the two brothers are equally sympathetic. Stewart plays the good brother with a dangerous edge, while Murphy's bad brother is impishly charming.

In 1955, British novelist Graham Greene published a book called *The Quiet American*, a scathing attack on American policy in Southeast Asia. The book's major characters include an American, a hopelessly naïve idealist; and an Englishman, an intellectual, extremely facile with words, who exhibits an existentialist objectivity which supposedly gives him an insight into the reality of the situation that the American lacks. The third principal character is a South Vietnamese woman caught between the two men and their ideas. The Englishman wants her as his mistress, the American, as his wife. As the book opens, the American has been found murdered, and the reason for his murder is seen in flashback through the eyes of the Englishman, who we gradually learn has realized that the American must die, and becomes an accomplice to the Communists who assassinated him.[528] Two years later, Joseph Mankiewicz made the novel into a movie. The basic plot remains the same, but in Mankiewicz's version, the now jaded Englishman has become a dupe of the Communists and participates in the crime merely to keep the innocent American from winning the girl. Together, the two treatments form an allegory for the dilemma of the political situation in Southeast Asia. Mankiewicz chose Audie Murphy as the ideal actor to portray his American. It was a good choice. Sue Gossett reports that one reviewer wrote that "Audie Murphy, with his fine war record and quiet charm, seemed perfectly cast in the role," and another, that, "Joseph Mankiewicz gets from Murphy a very interesting and mettlesome performance...."[529] However, the novel and the movie both portray extreme views, and the movie is as distorted in its anti-communism as the novel is in its anti-Americanism. Both novel and movie were quite controversial, and the movie suffered as well from the indifference of the American public of 1957 to the situation in Southeast Asia. Still, it was an interesting change of pace for Murphy, who more than held his own against the Englishman, played by Michael Redgrave. In the book, the American's naivete is seen to be more and more sinister, but in Murphy's hands, the same character gains more stature as the story deepens. The Englishman's cynical wit becomes petulant. It is a credit to Murphy's talent that he was so often able to portray a naïve innocent, when Murphy, the man, was neither. He had lost his innocence on the battlefield, and although he portrays a naïve American quite believably in this film, he returned from Saigon very disturbed by what he saw there. So much so that he "emptied his entire bank account into [a Saigon orphanage],"[530] In later years, during the height of the Vietnam war, he would recall to a reporter that he came back, "with the distinct impression that the South Vietnamese didn't care who ran that country," that he "often wonder[ed] why we cared enough to send our troops over there and kill off so many of our fine young men."[531] But the tragic figure in both treatments of the story is the Vietnamese girl, Phuong, who is seen by Greene as one "who only wants enough rice,"[532] and who returns to his bed as soon as the American is killed. Mankiewicz's Phoung shuns the Englishman, but when her husband-to-be is murdered, her only option is to go back to dancing for patrons in a bar, a short step from prostitution. Either way, she is a powerless victim who cannot control her own destiny. The public reaction of indifference to her plight is another example of the growing trend toward the repression of the warrioring instinct.

Murphy's next movie was a total departure from the seriousness of "The Quiet American," a delightful parody of his early "bad boy" films called "Ride a Crooked Trail." His friend "Spec" McClure reports a couple of incidents that took place on the Universal lot at that time. In one, Murphy and "Spec" happened to run into Murphy's attorney and his agent who were talking together. Murphy disturbed them by inquiring, "What are you stealing?" continuing with, "When two thieves get together they are bound to be stealing something." When "Spec" later asked Murphy what he had been referring to, the reply was, "I don't know. But they'll spend the rest of the day trying to guess what I've found out." Around the same time, Murphy mentioned to "Spec" that he was concerned about acting with his co-star in "Ride a Crooked Trail," the accomplished veteran, Walter Matthau. "Spec" joked to him that he should be more concerned about the boy and dog in the picture, who were both so adorable that they would be more likely to steal his scenes. Murphy's secretary apparently overheard the discussion, and wrote a change in the script that called for Murphy's character to shoot the boy and the dog. "The script change was meant a a private joke between us three," wrote McClure, "But Audie thought it was too good to waste. He sent the change through official channels until it reached the producer. The studio, never knowing whether to take Audie seriously or not, raised hell."[533]

Then, in another break from the Western, he played in "The Gun Runners," a remake of "To Have and Have Not," the Hemingway story originally brought to the screen by Humphrey Bogart and Lauren Bacall. Not only was this movie not a Western, but it explored a side to Murphy's talent seldom seen on screen, that of the lover. Gossett's book indicates that the critics saw his performance as "strongly appealing," and that he "[brought] an unexpected playfulness to the bedroom scenes that [was] very winning."[534]

But it is in his next two roles for Universal that the public could see quite strongly that it was a mistake to assume that Murphy was merely a personality projecting himself on the screen. Taken together, the two movies prove the error of confusing an actor's screen persona with the individual doing the acting. In "No Name on the Bullet," Murphy is coldly effective as a hired gunman who kills for a living. John Gant is a highly intelligent man who plays an "interesting game of Chess" and who seems to have justified, at least in his own mind, his chosen career. The most compelling part of his portrayal comes from his eyes, and the resignation they express, but that resignation is echoed in his stance, the cut of his shoulders, and the placidity of his demeanor as well. The movie succeeds because, somehow, Murphy manages to make the character seem sympathetic. He tells the town doctor, played by his friend Charles Drake, that "the real sicknesses, the most important ones, are seldom physical." He continues, "I believe I know more about those than you do." In Murphy's eyes we see the heart-sickness of those who have been through the dark journey of battle, as described by Joseph Campbell in *Hero with a Thousand Faces*. And yet, in his next movie, "The Wild and the Innocent," filmed within a month, we are charmed by the innocence and wonder of the mountain boy,

Yancey Hawkes, as he sees a city for the first time. And once again, it is not only Murphy's eyes which lead us into the character, it is his whole demeanor. And we watch, fascinated, as that look and that demeanor change when the youth comes face to face with the reality of civilization and its illusions. Murphy is able to portray this character because, like Yancey, he is more hunter than warrior. To a hunter, killing animals is one thing, killing human beings is another, as John Ehle writes in *Trail of Tears: The Rise and Fall of the Cherokee Nation*, "...the warrior's ways...were different from those of the hunter. While the hunter sought kinship with other creatures and offered salutation to those he must kill, the warrior was a brutal instrument of vengeance, the deliverer of death to others."[535] Joseph Campbell points out that the warrior is a product of civilization as opposed to the hunter who is nurtured in the natural world. Although Murphy accepted the necessity of killing during the war, he never completely developed the heart of a warrior. Like his character, Yancey Hawkes, he was willing to do what had to be done, but he "did not like the way that [he] did it." Taking human life was something "[he] would be living with for a long time."[536]

Murphy would co-produce his next film, "Cast a Long Shadow." His characterization of an illegitimate waif turned alcoholic, turned petty tyrant was very effective, but his greatest role would come with the movie he made afterwards, "The Unforgiven." The movie was directed by John Huston, and starred Audrey Hepburn and Burt Lancaster. Murphy accepted third billing because he wanted to work with Huston again, and the role gave him an opportunity to show that his characterization of quiet, heroic individuals was a choice, not a necessity. In "The Unforgiven," Cash Zachary is not only a coward, but a bigot as well. Murphy has several highly emotional scenes in this film, which he carries off quite well, telling reporters that he credited Huston with pulling the "histrionic performance" out of him. Sue Gossett points out that the critics regarded him "as doing the best acting job in the picture."[537] Co-star John Saxon, who would also star with him in "Posse from Hell," two years later, spoke highly of Murphy's acting talent during an interview on TV's Entertainment Tonight in 1989, saying, "...there was a great deal of truth in the way he did things."[538] There are two scenes in particular where he is outstanding. In one, he sees a Kiowa lance like the one that killed his father when he was a child, and completely loses control, firing blindly and crying at the same time. It is this moment in the film that gives sympathy to the character, where we learn that his swaggering machismo and hatred for the Kiowa is a cover-up for a fear that has been eating at him since childhood. And later, when he confronts his mother with knowledge of the "awful secret" that she has kept for years, that his younger sister (Audrey Hepburn) is herself a Kiowa, his tightly controlled rage is masterful. At the end of the movie, Cash overcomes his fear, and returns to save his family from a massacre at the hands of those same Indians, who had come to reclaim their sister, but his portrayal would have had the same strength regardless of the outcome. Murphy's role in this movie may have only received third billing, but it was clearly the pivotal role for the film. He considered this role the best in his career.

Although several of the characters he portrayed during these years may have been villainous or cowardly, the message of the films remained uplifting. Murphy's sense of responsibility, combined with the recognition and acceptance of the fact that he was considered a role model, led him to limit the roles he accepted to films with a positive impact. He might occasionally play the "bad guys," but never if they won. His characters inevitably dealt with the consequences of their actions by the final scene, in one way or another. Like Campbell's "supreme hero," he recognized his duty as a "keeper of the Law."

8
Songwriter

During the time Murphy was working on his autobiography, *To Hell and Back*, he often stayed awake nights, writing poetry. Few of those poems survive, but during the 1960's he turned that skill into a rewarding and profitable sideline. He wrote lyrics for Country and Western songs. It all began one evening when he and several friends, including recording artist Scott Turner were sitting around his den. The result of that first evening was his first hit song, "Shutters and Boards," which he and Turner wrote together. That song was first performed by Jerry Wallace, and later picked up by Dean Martin, Jimmy Dean, and several others. Today, there are over 60 versions of the song that have been recorded. Shortly afterwards, the two men wrote "When the Wind Blows in Chicago," which was recorded by Roy Clark. During that same year he wrote "Leave the Weeping to the Willow Tree," recorded by Bonnie Guitar. The next year, Wilton and Weldon released "Go on and Break my Heart," and Roy Clark, "My Lonesome Room." In all, he and Turner collaborated on 15 songs and instrumentals, and Charlie Pride recorded his last song, "Was it all Worth Losing You," which he wrote alone, in 1970.[539] He also collaborated with such artists as Jimmy Bryant, Sugar Rey, and Guy Mitchell. Although they never officially wrote a song together, he also frequently played around with lyrics with Marty Robbins.

The frightened boy who had trembled, in 1945, whenever he was forced to make a speech, had become an accomplished public speaker, and made the rounds of various organizations, especially during the 1960's, when he began speaking out on issues that were important to him. During one of those speeches, in 1968, at the dedication of the Alabama War Memorial, he recited his last poem, "Dusty Old Helmet."[540]

Murphy apparently derived much personal satisfaction from these poems and songs. They were usually composed during quiet evenings at home, when he and his friends were simply sitting around and visiting. During one of those evenings, according to Harold Simpson, Scott Turner had brought one of Murphy's favorite artists, Jerry Reed, along with him. The two men were mutual admirers, and both looked forward to meeting, but Turner had warned Reed not to bring up Murphy's war experiences. Murphy didn't like discussing them. However, after several hours of singing and playing, Murphy, in a rare mood, talked to Reed in some detail about the war.[541]

Country music, like myth, is a primary form of art. Based on simple folk rhythms and lyrics, it strikes a cord deep within our collective unconscious. Like Murphy himself, it is of the people, a straightforward reflection on life.

Larryann Willis, Executive Director of the Audie Murphy Research Foundation, recently posted one of Murphy's unpublished songs on the A&E Biography Message Boards, at www.biography.com. That song illustrates better, in Murphy's own words, the poignancy of his life, than any observation could.

MARIA'S FIRST ROSE

Dirty Helmet, shiny gun
Weary men too tired to run
Little girl on sandy shores
Watching solders go to war.

Lonely face not yet five years
Battle scarred and lined with fear
Little girl too young to die
Never knowing reasons why.

Little lady your sweet smile
Helps me down my dusty mile
Take my rose it's all I give
Please take it with my love in hopes that you
       might live.

Tiny hand takes lonely rose
From stranger that she'll never know
Tearful eyes see soldier cry
As he turns to wave good-bye.

The little girl's grown older now
Wars have gone away
Still the rose within a page
Forever brings back memories that were
    yesterdays.

Dirty helmet, shiny gun
Weary men too tired to run.
Little girl on sandy shores
Watching soldiers go to war.

-Audie Murphy[542]

9
The Last Real Action Hero

In late 1958, Universal-International began taking steps that would lead to a merger in 1962 with MCA (Music Corporation of America).[543] They began by selling the back lot and its sound stages to MCA to be used primarily for television productions. Universal had been losing money on its Westerns. Audie Murphy was their only Western star whose movies continued to make a profit, and the studio decided it was time for Murphy to move to television.[544] They first suggested a series of stories about World War II, but Murphy understandably refused, so they decided on a Western series. "Whispering Smith" was to be a black-and-white half-hour format western.[545] Production on the series began in '59, shortly after Murphy returned from Mexico where he had been filming "The Unforgiven." Simultaneously with the TV series, the studios began a series of Western movies to be produced by Gordon Kay, all starring Audie Murphy, to be produced over a seven-year period to 1965, which extended his contract with the studio another three years from 1962. The movies were to make money by reducing production time and costs. The top priority was to get them in on time and under budget.[546] They took no risks with the Murphy "persona," since it had been successful in the past. The concept worked financially, but gave Murphy little opportunity to expand his acting potential. The same was true for most of the movies he made outside the studio during the Sixties, which were either westerns or adventure stories. Meantime, the TV series was a disaster. MCA assumed that they could bank on Murphy's popularity, and put little of any value into the series. Although NBC accepted the premise, there was some difficulty finding a sponsor, and though the show was supposed to air in fall of 1960, it was delayed until spring of '61.[547] By that time, half-hour westerns were appearing several times a night, every night of the week, and audiences were dropping them in favor of the hour to hour-and-a-half color series like "Bonanza" and "The Virginian." Murphy was quite vocal about his disappointment with the series, saying, when it finally aired, "It's like the Redstone rocket, obsolete, but they're going to fire it anyway." Originally scheduled for 26 shows, it was cancelled after 13. Murphy was relieved, and said so publicly, even though the delay cost him a great deal of money at a very bad time.[548]

While he enjoyed making films, particularly Westerns, the roles he preferred to play grew harder and harder to come by. The themes of movies in general were changing. Hollywood shifted from fairy-tale endings to an existentialist realism. Instead of carrying the hero's story to its natural conclusion, they dropped the idea of heroism altogether. There were no good guys. Rollo May refers to this phenomenon as the "collapse of heroism."[549] "We make heroes out of gangsters," he wrote. "In the movies we identify with the criminal." He refers to "Dillinger," and to the hard-bitten characters often played by Clint Eastwood.[550] Murphy was still being offered roles, but they were roles he did not want to play. One of those roles was later given to Clint Eastwood. The movie was "A Fistful of Dollars."[551]

In 1967, Murphy told Thomas Morgan that he wanted to turn to producing.[552] He had co-produced several films already, and had learned that competing with television would require a large budget, and that meant major money. To get that kind of money involved taking major risks. Taking risks didn't bother him. He was still a hunter, and audacious risks were a hunter's stock-in-trade. They had served him well in the past. He knew about losses, but he had always won more than he had lost. He had made several profitable investments, but money had never been a priority.[553] The fun of gambling was in the challenge. He had one "flaw" that would hinder him during this time. Unless he was in a real battle, he couldn't, or wouldn't, go for the jugular. He cared too much for people to use them. Like his movie personae, he couldn't shoot people in the back. He knew that every gambler goes through periods of losses, and was prepared to see them through. If he went through a few lean years, he wouldn't be dealing with anything new. He had been broke before and had survived. The most important goal was to be clear of the studio system. Eventually, the risks would pay off. Besides, Audie Murphy was a fatalist. The lessons of warfare had taught him that a soldier's survival depended on his luck rather than his skill. But he wasn't gambling simply because he thought his luck might make him rich. Murphy didn't care that much about being rich. He was even known to have deliberately lost a windfall at the race track because he thought it might bring him *bad* luck.[554]

But compounding the financial problems, his insomnia and continuing nightmares worsened. Eventually he turned to prescription sleeping pills, which were supposed to be non-addictive. They weren't. At first they worked, but he began needing more and more of them. His behavior was changing. He was becoming more and more volatile. The quality of his work was suffering. It was not long before he realized that the pills were the problem and stopped taking them. He found himself, to his surprise, going through withdrawal symptoms. He knew he was hooked. This problem took a different kind of courage, but he won the battle. He stopped taking pills.[555]

Realizing how easy it was to become addicted, he went public, appeared on several TV shows, and gave interviews, and told about his addiction and his struggle with what is now called post-traumatic stress disorder, or PTSD. Never having chosen, much less relished, his hero status, it was not important to him that his reputation might suffer. He was more concerned with the good it might do for others to know.

And then, there was Vietnam. From the time of the Korean conflict he had been concerned with the concept of limited warfare.[556] Anyone who had spent four months on Anzio would have to have been. He was also concerned with the growing devaluation of the warrior.[557] You could say he opposed the war, but upheld the warrior. This stand made him unpopular with elements on both sides. The Hawks considered him a traitor, and could not understand why he refused to support their cause. Doves, on the other hand, knew of his war record, and heard only his comments about the importance of accepting the men who were fighting. He worked especially hard to have the government recognize its responsibility in treating mental wounds of war as well as physical ones. And he could not help but realize that in this war, the young men doing the fighting were usually poor, often from minority groups.

We have already seen that a hero who cannot step down becomes a tyrant. Some who do not become tyrants, according to Campbell, become ascetics, or monks, and retire from public life.[558] The knight Percival was one of these. When he had found the Grail, he retired with his family to a castle deep in the forest, and neither he nor the Grail was seen again. But as Emma Jung and Marie-Louise von Franz point out in *The Grail Legend*, when he retreated, Arthur's Round Table disintegrated.[559] Audie Murphy could not become an ascetic any more than he could become a tyrant. Campbell goes on to say that the hero's only other option is to become a "redeemer," a martyr to his cause, sacrificing himself to support the message that is no longer being heeded.[560] It comes as no surprise that this is the path Murphy took. He did not want young men going to war holding his name up as heroic. By going public with his problems, he made himself a target for a media that had already turned against him.

He continued to fight for his concept of justice, including his battle against drug traffic. As early as 1956 word leaked through the press that he had taken part in several "stings" which had resulted in convictions of drug dealers.[561] Pieces of information surfaced in the press over the years, mostly in the early years after his death, that indicate he had continued to work with law enforcement agencies at one level or another after 1956.[562] *Time Magazine*, in his obituary, indicated he had been working with the Los Angeles District Attorney's office, gathering information on cases involving organized crime.[563] But for the most part, this was a very private area of Murphy's life, one that even his closest friends were not aware of.

By the late 1960's, he had begun finding the means to turn his financial situation around. He poured everything he could get together into producing a Western with Budd Boetticher, a movie ironically called "A Time for Dying."[564] In an effort to finance the completion of this film, Murphy acted as a middleman on a real estate transaction for which he was to receive a finder's fee. He met with the property owners and investors in Atlanta, and together they took off in a small plane for Virginia. A few miles short of their destination, the pilot radioed in that they were in bad weather. The plane then disappeared. Three days later the wreckage was found near the top of a mountain outside Roanoke. There were no survivors.[565]

10
Departure

Major Audie Leon Murphy was buried with full military honors at Arlington Cemetery. The headstone on his grave is simple Government Issue, with no adornments. He would have preferred something even simpler, a private funeral attended only by his family.

Near the crash site on the mountain there is a small monument. In spite of its remoteness, it is visited often.

There are historical markers in Kingston, Celeste, and Farmersville, all proclaiming the honor of being his birthplace. The number of memorials, statues, and commemorations continues to grow.

All of this is fitting for a mythic hero, who invariably dies mysteriously, and who had multiple shrines honoring the sites of his birth, death, and burial, and Murphy is, without doubt, a hero of mythic proportions.

But there was little national mourning for this hero at the time of his death. Like many before him, he had passed from favor; his country had all but forgotten him. Some said he died a failure - in poverty. Some said he had gambled away a fortune. But there were as many indications that his financial situation was a temporary one, that he was recovering his losses, and had plans to continue producing movies, outside the studio system.

Even if it is true that he was in such debt, to consider his life a failure is to put a financial value on success. Rollo May writes of the tendency for Americans to get caught up in what he calls "the Horatio Alger myth." May connects this myth to the influence of Calvinism in our culture, saying, "The man of wealth was therefore the good man, for his wealth showed that God approved of him."[566] This myth has such a strong influence on our time that people see those who are not obviously successful financially as failures at living. But Horatio Alger was not Audie Murphy's myth. The quest for material wealth was in total opposition to the lessons he had learned during the journey, the message he was trying to relate, but which was going unheeded. He had a family and friends who thought highly of him, who mourned his loss. He accepted the hero's responsibility and delivered the message, and though few people listened during his life, it is not too late to remember.

Murphy taught us to win with humility, lose without complaining, to fight when fighting was necessary, but at the same time, "never hurt others willingly, including ourselves." He told us that unfaced fear leads to "selfishness, cruelty, and lack of self-respect." He emphatically insisted that "we are our brother's keeper." His words can perhaps best be summed up by saying that what is important is not how much you take from the world, but how much you contribute to it. But Audie Murphy did more that tell us how we ought to live, he lived that way himself. He was a quietly generous man who shared what he had with others; he was humble, and made light of his own heroism, talents, and successes, he valued his family, he chose friends according to what they were rather that according to what they could do for him. He was honest, he accepted responsibility even when it was thrust upon him, as a child, as a soldier, and as a man, he protected others by putting himself in the line of fire, not only in battle, but in his later life as well.

Audie Murphy would agree with Joseph Campbell's conclusions to *Hero with a Thousand Faces*. Campbell warns us that while it is important to honor and remember the hero, we should not take the symbol literally. The archetypes are "symbols to be contemplated" rather than "examples to imitate."[567] We do not have to literally go to war to learn the lesson of the warrior. We only have to look in the mirror and accept what we see. Our dark journeys should be an exploration of the darkness within ourselves, and the treasure we find there will enable us to integrate the shadow side of our own personalities rather than projecting it on to others. If we can do that, we might eventually be able to eliminate the need for war altogether. While going to war taught Murphy the great lessons of life, it also created severe psychic wounds that never healed. Today we understand more about the devastating effects of war on the soldier's psyche, but after World War II, "few sought treatment for their symptoms or discussed the emotional effects of their wartime experiences. Society expected them to put it all behind them, forget the war, and get on with their lives."[568] His friend, jockey Jay Fishburn called him "the last American hero," and added, "Audie knew a lot of people, but he never got really close to anyone. There was a wall you couldn't get behind. It's like he had been somewhere nobody else had gone and you couldn't go with him."[569] Campbell ends *Hero with a Thousand Faces* by telling us that the hero should be honored, "not in the moments of his tribes great victories, but in the silences of his personal despair."[570] Let us so remember Audie Murphy.

Bibliography

Allen, William L. *Anzio: Edge of Disaster*. NY: Elsevier-Dutton, 1978.

American Psychiatric Association. *DSM-IV: Daignostic and Statistical Manual of Mental Disorders*. Washington,D. C.: American Psychiatric Association, 1994.

Arnold, Maxine. "The Personal War of Audie Murphy." *Photoplay*. October 1955: 59-62,108-110.

Audie Leon Murphy Memorial Website. www.audiemurphy.com, 1998.

"Audie Murphy." *Movie Fan*. July 1952: 20-21.

"Battle for the Boot." *Masters of War*. The History Channel. 11 July 1998.

"Behind the scenes with 'Walk the Proud Land'." *Screen Stories*. October 1956: 48.

Bly, Robert. *Iron John*. NY: Vintage Books, 1992.

Butcher, Henry C. *My Three Yearws with Eisenhower*. New York: Simon and Schuster, 1946.

Campbell, Joseph. *Flight of the Wild Gander*. New York: Harper Perennial, 1990.

Campbell, Joseph. *Hero with a Thousand Faces*. 3 ed. Princeton: Princeton University Press, 1968.

Campbell, Joseph. *The Masks of God: Creative Mythology*. NY: Penguin Books, 1987.

Campbell, Joseph. *The Masks of God: Primitive Mythology*. NY: Penguin Books, 1986.

Campbell, Joseph. *The Power of Myth*. NY: Doubleday, 1988.

Campbell, Joseph. *Transformations of Myth Through Time*. 1 ed. NY: Harper and Row, 1990.

Campbell, Randolph B. *Gone to Texas: A History of the Lone Star State*. NY: Oxford University Press. 2003.

Chodorow, Nancy J. *Feminism and Psychoanalytic Theory*. NY: Yale University Press, 1989.

"Destry." Dir. George Marshall. With Audie Murphy, Mari Blanchard, and Thomas Mitchell. Universal-International Studios, 1954.

Dorian, Bob. "Bob Dorian's Classic Hollywood." *American Movie Classics Magazine*. June 1997: n.pag.

Edwards, Ralph. "This is Your Life, Audie Murphy." *Photoplay*. June 1954: 56-57,94-97.

Ehle, John. *The Trail of Tears: The Rise and Fall of the Cherokee Nation*. NY: Anchor Books. 1988/

Eisler, Riane. *The Chalice and the Blade*. NY: HarperCollins Publishers, 1988.

Eliot, Thomas S. *Four Quartets*. San Diego: Harcourt, Brace Jovanovich, 1971.

"The Empire Strikes Back." Dir. Irvin Kershner. With Mark Hamill, Harrison Ford, and Carrie Fisher. 20th Century Fox, 1980.

"The Enemy Within." <u>Star Trek</u>. Prod. Paramount. 1966.

"Facts about Post-Traumatic Stress Disorder." National Institute of Mental Health Publication No. OM-99 4157 September 1999. www.nimh.gov

Fishburn, Jay. *Audie Murphy Research Foundation Newsletter.* 2 (1997): 1-2.

Flynn, Stephen. "Analysis of Snow Whie and the Seven Dwarfs." *The G. G. Jung Page.* www.cgjungpage.org.

Foulke, Robert, and Paul Smith. *Elements of Literature: Sixth Course.* "The Romance." Ed. Robert Anderson and others. New York: Holt, Rinehart, and winston, Inc, 1989.

Gossett, Sue. *The Films and Career of Audie Murphy.* 2 ed. Madison, NC: Empire Publishing Company, 1997.

Greene, Graham. *The Quiet American: Text and Criticism.* Ed. John C. Pratt. NY: Penguin Books, 1996.

Guches, Richard C., Ed.D. *Sequel: A Handbook for the Critical Analysis of Literature.* 5 ed. Palo Alto: Peek Publications, 1985.

Gunsmoke. Dir. Nathan Juran. With Audie Murphy, Susan Cabot, and Charles Drake. Universal-International Studios, 1953.

Herman, Judith, M. D. *Trauma and Recovery.* 2 ed. NY: BasicBooks, 1997.

Holliday, Kate. "Still in Stride." *Screenland.* April 1949: 49, 64-65.

Hubler, Richard G. "He Doesn't Want to be a Star." *Saturday Evening Post.* 18 April 1953: 34-35,153-155,158.

Hutchings, Peter. *Approaches to Popular Film.* Ed. Joanne Hollows and Mark Jancovich. NY: Manchester University Press, 1995.
"Inside Story." *Entertainment Tonight.* 1989.
"James Cagney Biography." *Baseline Encyclopedia of Film.* Cinemania Microsoft Corporation 1993
Jung, Carl. *Man and his Symbols.* New York: Dell Publishing Company, 1968.
Jung, Carl G. *The Collected Works, Vol. 9: The Archetypes and the Collective Unconscious.* 2 ed. Trans. R. F. C. Hull. Princeton: Princeton University Press, 1980.
Jung, Carl G. *The Collected Works, Vol 5: Symbols of Transformation.* Princeton: Princeton University Press, 1976.
Jung, Emma, and Marie-Louise von Franz. *The Grail Legend.* Boston: Sigo Press, 1986.
Klein, Edward N. "Audie Murphy Did a Lot More than Win a Bunch of Medals." *Hudson Valley Business Journal.*
Liddell Hart, B. H. *History of the Second World War.* NY: G. P. Putnam's Sons, 1970.
Little Big Man. Dir. Arthur Penn. With Dustin Hoffman and Chief Dan George. Cinema Center Film, 1970.
"The Man Who Lived Twice." *Screen album.* May-July 1956: n.pag.
"Matinee Classics." Narr. Nick Clooney. American Movie Classics. 1997.
May, Rollo. *The Cry for Myth.* 2 ed. New York: Delta, 1992.

McClure, David. "Audie Murphy: Man of Humor." (unpublished article).

McClure, David. "Audie Murphy: The Man." (unpublished article).

McClure, David. "How Audie Murphy became a Movie Star." *Movieland*. 1955

McCurdy, Jole C. *Psyche's Stories*. 1 ed. "The Structural and Archetypal analysis of Fairy Tales." Ed. Murray Stein and Lionel Corbett. Wilmette: Chiron Publications, 1991.

Moore, Viola. "They're Doing All They Can." *Motion Picture*. April 1050: 40-41,67.

Morgan, Thomas B. "The War Hero." Esquire. December 1983: 597-604.

Morison, Samuel E. *History of United States Naval Operations in World War II, Volume IX, Sicily, Salerno, Anzio*. Boston: Little Brown and Company, 1954.

Murphy, Audie. 'I'd Rather Return.' *Audie Murphy Reserach Foundation Newsletter*. 4 (1998): 1-8.

Murphy, Audie. 'Less that a Year.' *Audie Murphy Research Foundation Newsletter*. 3 (1998): 3.

Murphy, Audie. To Hell and Back. NY: MJF Books, 1977.

Murphy, Audie. "You Do the Prayin' and I'll Do the Shootin'." *Modern Screen*. January 1956: 60.

Murphy, Audie L. "Lt Audie Murphy Knows what GI Wants--And it isn't War." *Dallas Times Herald*. 7 July 1945: : n.pag.

Murphy, Edward F. *Heroes of WWII*. 2 ed. New York: Ballantine Books, 1992.

Murphy, Terry. "Interview with Charles L. Owen." *Audie Murphy Research Foundation Newsletter*. 1 (1997): 2-6.

"Murphy Will Appear for Opening of 'Hell'." *Dallas Times Herald*. 14 August 1955 sec. 8: 1.

Pearson, Carol, Ph. D. *Awakening the Heroes Within*. San Francisco: Harper, 1991.

Pearson, Carol S., Ph. D. *The Hero Within*. 2 ed. NY: HarperCollis Publishers, 1989.

"PTSD and Older Veterans: A National Center for PTSD Fact Sheet." National Center for Post-Traumatic Stress Disorder, Department of Veterans Affairs. www.ncptsd.va.gov

"Rancher Audie Murphy." *TV Radio Mirror*. June 1961: 45-48.

Return of the Jedi. Dir. Richard Marquand. With Mark Hamill, Harrison Ford, and Carrie Fisher. 20th Century Fox, 1983.

Riley, Vicki. "Journey into Light." *Photoplay*. February 1957: 56-57,83-85.

Schnurr, Paula P. "PTSD and Combat-Related Psychiatric Symptoms in Older Veterans." *PTSD Research Quarterly*. Volume 2, Number 1. Winter 1991

Scott, John L. "Audie Murphy, No. 1 Hero, Slogs Again." *Los Angeles Times*. 5 September 1955

Sheehan, Fred. *Anzio: Epic of Bravery*. Norman: University of Oklahoma Press, 1994.

Simpson, Harold B. *Audie Murphy: American Soldier*. Dallas: Alcor Publishing Company, 1982.

Squire, Charles. *Celtic Myth and Legend: Poetry and Romance*. Van Nuys: Newcastle Publishing Co., 1975.

Thomas, Tony. *The Best of Universal*. 1 ed. Vestal, NY: The Vestal Press, Ltd, 1990.

"Time of Decision." *Silver Screen*. February 1956: 56-57.

"To Hell and Not Quite Back." *Time*. 14 July 1971

Tuska, John. *The American West in Film: Critical Approaches to the Western*. Westport, Connecticut: Greenwood Press, 1985.

United States Government. *Hearings before the Subcommittee in the Federal Criminal Code of the Committee on the Judiciary, United States Senate*. Washington: Government Printing Office, 1956.

"Universal Pictures." *Baseline's Encyclopedia of Film*. Cinemania Microsoft Corporation. 1993.

von Franz, Marie-Louise. *Projection and Recollection in Jungian Psychology*. London: Open Court, 1993.

Washburn, Phillip T. "Audie Murphy: Actor, Songwriter, Soldier." *Ft. Hood Sentinel*. 16 January 1997

The Wild and the Innocent. Dir. Jack Sher. With Audie Murphy, Sandra Dee, and Gilbert Roland. Universal-International Studios, 1959.

Wilkie, Jane. "Memoirs of a Small Texan." *Modern Screen*. July 1955: 58, 85-86.

Willis, Larryann, Ex. Dir. Lecture. www.biography.com. Audie Murphy Research Foundation. n.p. 5 Sept 1998.

"World in My Corner." Dir. Jesse Hibbs. With Audie Murphy, John McIntire, and Barbara Rush. Universal-International Studios,

ENDNOTES

[2] May, Rollo *The Cry for Myth* (New York: Delta Publishing 1991) 33 (emphasis added)

[3] May 54

[4] Campbell, Joseph. *Hero with a Thousand Faces* (Princeton: Princeton University Press 1973) 245

[5] Eliot, T. S. "Little Gidding." *Four Quartets* (San Diego: Harcourt Brace Jovanovich 1971) 59

[6] McCurdy, Jole Capiello, "The Structural and Archetypal Analysis of Fairy Tales," *Psyche's Stories,* ed. Murray Stein and Lionel Corbett, (Wilmott, Illinois: Chiron Publications) 1991 4-8

[7] McCurdy 9

[8] McCurdy 8-10

[9] Guches, Richard C. "Psychological and Archetypal Analysis" Sequel: A Handbook for the Critical Analysis of Literature (Palo Alto: Peek Publications 1985) 120

[10] Jung, Carl G. "Symbols of Transformation" *The Collected Works of C. G. Jung* Vol. 5 (Princeton: Princeton University Press 1976) 228

[11] May 15

[12] Campbell. *Hero* 249

[13] May 58

[14] Flynn, Stephen, "Analysis of Snow White and the Seven Dwarfs," *The C. G. Jung Page*, www.cgjungpage.org. 2005.

[15] Guches 127

[16] McCurdy 14

[17] Campbell *Hero* 37

[18] Pearson, Carol *The Hero Within* (San Francisco: HarperCollins Publishers 1989) 5

[19] May 58

[20] Guches 124

[21] May 58

INTRODUCTION Chapter 1: Primordial Background

[22] Campbell, Joseph *Primitive Mythology* 241

[23] Chodorow, Nancy *Feminism and Psychoanalytic Theory* (New York: Yale University Press 1989) 24

[24] Campbell *Primitive* 136

[25] Chodorow 24

[26] Eisler, Riane *The Chalice and the Blade* (New York: HarperCollins Publishers 1988) 14

[27] Chodorow 24

[28] Eisler 44

INTRODUCTION Chapter 2: The Hero as Warrior

[29] Campbell; *Hero* 337-338

[30] Campbell *Hero* 337

[31] Pearson 75

INTRODUCTION Chapter 3: The Childhood of the Mythological Hero

[32] Campbell. *Hero 326*

[33] Guches 124

[34] Pearson 4

[35] Campbell *Hero 327*

[36] von Franz, Marie Louise *Projection and Recollection in Jungian Psychology* (London: Open Court 1993)78

[37] May 20

[38] von Franz 78; May 38

[39] von Franz 79

[40] May 20

[41] May 38

INTRODUCTION Chapter 4: The Childhood of Audie Murphy

[42] Murphy, Edward F. *Heroes of WWII* (New York: Ballantine Books 1990) 263

[43] Murphy, Audie. *To Hell and Back* (New York: MFJ Books 1977) 7

[44] Simpson 17

[45] Gossett, Sue *The Films and Career of Audie Murphy* (Madison, NC: Empire Publishing Company 1997) 7

[46] Simpson 25

[47] Hubler, Richard. "He Doesn't Want to be a Star." *Saturday Evening Post* 18 April 1953 153

[48] Hubler 154

[49] Hubler 153

[50] Murphy, Edward F. 263

[51] Simpson 20

[52] Murphy, Edward F. 262

[53] Simpson 22

[54] Simpson 17

[55] Simpson, 28

[56] Murphy, Edward F. 264

[57] Hubler 153

[58] Murphy, Audie *To Hell* 7

[59] Simpson 20

[60] Murphy, Audie. *To Hell 141*

[61] Murphy, Audie *To Hell* 7

[62] Simpson 22

[63] Kellar, Brad "Nadine Murphy Recalls Her Older Brother, Audie" *Greenville Herald Banner* May 18 1997

[64] Gossett 7

[65] Simpson 26

[66] Murphy, Audie. "You Do the Prayin' and I'll Do the Shootin'," *Modern Screen* Jan 1956 60

[67] Hubler 154

[68] Murphy, Audie "You Do" 61

[69] Murphy, Audie "You Do" 61.

[70] Campbell. *Hero* 327

[71] Gossett 7

BOOK I – The Hero's Journey - Part 1, Chapter 1: The Call to Adventure

[72] Campbell, Joseph *Hero with a Thousand Faces* (Princeton: Princeton University Press 1973) 58

[73] Campbell *Hero* 62

[74] Murphy, Audie "You Do the Prayin' and I'll Do the Shootin'." *Modern Screen* Jan 1956 60

[75] Murphy, Audie *To Hell and Back* 6

BOOK 1 Part 1 – Chapter 2: Supernatural Aid

[76] Campbell *Hero* 69

[77] Simpson, Harold *Audie Murphy: American Soldier* (Dallas: Alcor Publishing Company 1982) 45

[78] Washburn, Phillip T. "Audie Murphy: Actor, Songwriter, Soldier" *Fort Hood Sentinel* 16 Jan 1977 reprinted: Audie L. Murphy Memorial Website

[79] "Little Big Man" dir. Arthur Penn with Dustin Hoffman, Chief Dan George Cinema Center Films 1970

[80] Simpson 22

[81] Simpson 22

[82] Simpson 49

BOOK I Part 1 – Chapter 3: Crossing the First Threshold

[83] Campbell *Hero* 51

[84] Campbell *Hero* 78

[85] Murphy, Audie *To Hell and Back* (New York: MJF Books 1977) 8

[86] Murphy, Audie *To Hell* 8

[87] Morgan, Thomas B. "The War Hero." *Esquire* Dec 1983 604

[88] Murphy, Audie *To Hell* 8

[89] Simpson 49

[90] Campbell *Hero* 92

[91] Simpson 54

BOOK I Part 2 – Chapter 4: The Belly of the Whale

[92] Murphy, Audie "Lt. Audie Murphy Knows what G. I. Wants - And it Isn't War" told to William Barnard in *Dallas Times Herald* July 7, 1945

[93] Simpson 66

[94] Simpson 67

[95] Simpson 67

[96] Simpson 68

BOOK I Part 2 – Introduction: The Road of Trials

[97] Campbell, Joseph *Hero with a Thousand Faces* (Princeton: Princeton University Press 1977) 97

BOOK I Part 2 Chapter 1: Sicily

[98] Campbell, Joseph *Hero with a Thousand Faces* *(Princeton: Princeton University Press* 1973) 245

[99] Morison, Samuel E. *History of Naval Operations in World War Two*, Vol. IX,"Sicily, Salerno, Anzio (Boston: Little Brown and company 1954) 68-69

[100] Allen, William L. *Anzio: Edge of Disaster* (New York: Elsevier-Dutton 1978)8

[101] Morison 10

[102] Liddell Hart, B. H. *History of the Second World War* (New York: G. P. Putnam's Sons 1970)439

[103] Morison 20

[104] Simpson, Harold *Audie Murphy: American Soldier* (Dallas: Alcor Publishing Company 1975) 68

[105] Murphy, Edward F. *Heroes of WWII* (New York: Ballantine Books 1990)102

[106] Liddell Hart 440

[107] Morison 26

[108] Simpson 68

[109] Morison 19

[110] Simpson 69

[111] Morison 78

[112] Butcher, Henry C. *My Three Years with Eisenhower: The Personal Diary of Captain Harry C. Butcher,*

USNR Naval Aide to General Eisenhower, 1942-1945

337

[113] Morison 80

[114] Butcher 353

[115] Morison 86

[116] Simpson 69

[117] Simpson 69

[118] Murphy, Audie *To Hell* 1

[119] Morison 87

[120] Murphy, Edward F. 102-103

[121] Butcher 361

[122] Morison 173

[123] Murphy, Audie *To Hell* 11

[124] Murphy, Edward F. 103

[125] Morison 181

[126] Morison 183

[127] Murphy, Audie *To Hell* 12

[128] Morison 184

[129] Hubler, Richard "He Doesn't Want to be a Star."

Saturday Evening Post 18 April 1953 154

[130] Murphy, Audie *To Hell* 12

[131] Murphy, Audie *To Hell* 12

[132] Murphy, Audie *To Hell* 13

[133] Morison 196

[134] Morison 197

[135] Butcher 385

[136] Murphy, Audie *To Hell* 15

[137] Morison 200

[138] Butcher 389-390

[139] Murphy, Audie *To Hell* 15

[140] Murphy, Edward F. 110

BOOK I part 2 Chapter 2: Salerno to the Mignano Gap

[141] Allen, William L. *Anzio: Edge of Disaster* (New York Elsevier-Dutton 1978) 9

[142] Allen 10

[143] Allen 10

[144] Allen 16

[145] Murphy, Edward F. *Heroes of WWII* (New York: Ballantine Books 1990) 112

[146] Allen 15

[147] Liddell Hart, B. H.. *The History of the Second World War* (New York: B. H. Putnam and Sons 1970) 461

[148] Allen 15

[149] Allen 17

[150] Murphy, Edward F. 112

[151] Butcher 418

[152] Simpson, Harold *Audie Murphy: American Soldier* (Dallas: Alcor Publishing Company 1982) 85

[153] Murphy, Edward F. 117

[154] Simpson 87

[155] Simpson 87

[156] Murphy, Audie *To Hell* 15

[157] Murphy, Audie *To Hell* 18

[158] Simpson 87

[159] Murphy, Audie *To Hell* 22

[160] Murphy, Edward F. 118

[161] Simpson 88

[162] Murphy, Audie *To Hell* 26

[163] Murphy, Audie, *To Hell* 33

[164] Murphy, Audie *To Hell* 34

[165] Butcher 433

[166] Murphy, Edward F. 119

[167] Murphy, Audie *To Hell* 37

[168] Murphy, Audie *To Hell* 41

[169] McClure, David "How Audie Murphy Won His Medals, Part II" *Audie Murphy Research Foundation Newsletter,* Spring 1997 13

[170] Murphy, Audie *To Hell* 4

[171] Bly, Robert *Iron John* (New York: Vintage Books 1992) 156

[172] Murphy, Edward F. 119

BOOK I Part 2 Chapter 3: Naples

[173] Simpson, Harold. *Audie Murphy: American Soldier* (Dallas: Arcor Publishing Company 1982) 91

[174] Murphy, Audie. *To Hell* 51

[175] Simpson 91

[176] Murphy, Audie *To Hell* 52

[177] Murphy, Edward F. *Heroes of WWII* (New York, Ballantine 1990) 265

[178] Murphy, Audie *To Hell* 52

[179] Murphy, Audie *To Hell* 13

[180] Murphy, Audie *To Hell* 61

[181] Murphy, Audie *To Hell* 61

[182] Campbell, Joseph. *Hero with a Thousand Faces* (Princeton: Princeton University Press 1973) 111

[183] Murphy, Audie *To Hell* 78

BOOK I Part 2 Chapter 4: Anzio

[184] Campbell *Hero* 121

[185] "Battle for the Boot" *Masters of War* The History Channel July 11, 1998

[186] Allen, William. *Anzio: Edge of Disaster* New York: Elsevier-Dutton 1978) 24

[187] Morison, Samuel E. *History of Naval Operations in World War Two* vol IX "Sicily, Salerno, Anzio" (Boston: Little Brown and Company 1954) 318

[188] Sheehan, Fred *Anzio: Epic of Bravery* (Norman: University of Oklahoma Press 1994) 20

[189] Sheehan 24

[190] Butcher 465

[191] Murphy, Audie *Hell and To Back* (New York MJF Books 1977) 80

[192] Murphy, Audie *To Hell* 80

[193] Murphy, Edward F. *Heroes of WWII* (New York: Ballantine Books 1990) 126

[194] Sheehan 24

[195] Morison 353

[196] Murphy, Audie. *To Hell* 86

[197] Sheehan 67

[198] Morison 353

[199] Murphy, Audie *To Hell* 96

[200] Simpson 369

[201] Sheehan 67

[202] Murphy, Audie *To Hell* 99

[203] Morgan, Thomas B. "The War Hero." *Esquire* Dec 1983 603

[204] Murphy, Audie *To Hell* 100

[205] Sheehan 81

[206] Murphy, Audie *To Hell* 102

[207] Sheehan 81

[208] Sheehan 82

[209] Murphy, Audie *To Hell* 105

[210] Murphy, Audie *To Hell* 52

[211] Murphy, Audie *To Hell* 107

[212] Allen 77

[213] Allen 81

[214] Murphy, Audie *To Hell* 109

[215] Sheehan 88

[216] Murphy, Audie *To Hell* 109.

[217] Butcher 458

[218] Allen 125

[219] McClure, David "How Audie Murphy Won His Medals, Part II" *Audie Murphy Research Foundation Newsletter* Spring 1997 14

[220] Murphy, Audie *To Hell* 142

[221] Allen 127

[222] Murphy, Audie *To Hell* 146

[223223] Allen 128

[224] Murphy, Audie *To Hell* 115

[225] Murphy, Audie Letter to Beatrice Springfield. *Audie Murphy Research Foundation Newsletter* vol. 1 Winter 1977

[226] Murphy, Audie. *To Hell* 117

[227] Murphy, Audie *Dallas Times Herald* reprinted in the *Audie Murphy Research Foundation Newsletter* Spring 1998 2

[228] reprinted from *Audie L. Murphy Memorial Website* www.audiemurphy.com

[229] McClure, David "How Audie Murphy Won His Medals, Part II" 14

[230] Murphy, Edward F.131

[231] Murphy, Audie *To Hell* 146

[232] Sheehan, Fred 197

[233] McClure "How Audie Murphy Won His Medals, Part II" 14

[234] Murphy, Audie *To Hell* 150

[235] Sheehan 200

[236] Butcher 550

[237] Sheehan 206

[238] Murphy, Audie *To Hell* 162-3

BOOK I Part 2 Chapter 5: France

[239] Simpson, Harold *Audie Murphy: American Soldier* (Dallas: Alcor Publishing Company) 119

[240] Murphy, Edward F. *Heroes of WWII* (New York: Ballantine Books 1990) 216

[241] Murphy, Audie *To Hell and Back* (New York MJF Books 1977) 169

[242] Murphy, Audie *To Hell* 171-172

[243] Murphy, Audie *Dallas Times Herald* article July 1945 reprinted in the *Audie Murphy Research Foundation Newsletter* spring 1998 3

[244] McClure, David "How Audie Murphy Won His Medals, Part III" *Audie Murphy Research Foundation Newsletter* Winter 1998 5

[245] Reprinted from *Audie L. Murphy Memorial Website* www.audiemurphy.com

[246] Murphy, Audie *Dallas Times Herald* reprint 3

[247] Murphy, Audie *To Hell* 172

[248] Murphy, Audie *To Hell* 173-176

[249] Murphy, Edward F. 265

[250] Butcher 647

[251] Murphy, Edward F. 217

[252] Murphy, Audie *To Hell* 188-189

[253] Murphy, Audie *Audie Murphy Research Foundation Newsletter* Summer 1998

[254] "The Empire Strikes Back," dir. Irvin Kershner, Mark Hamill, Harrison Ford, Carrie fisher, Billy Dee Williams 20th Century Fox 1980

[255] "Return of the Jedi,' dir. Richard Marquand, Mark Hamill, Harrison Ford, Carrie Fisher, Billy Dee Williams 20th Century Fox 1983

[256] Campbell, Joseph. *Hero with a Thousand Faces* (Princeton: Princeton University Press 1972) 6

[257] Campbell *Hero* 147

[258] Campbell *Hero* 147

[259] von Franz, Marie-Louise *Projections and Recollections in Jungian Psychology* (London: Open Court 1993) p 123

[260] von Franz 2

[261] Murphy, Edward F. 222

[262] Simpson 129

[263] Murphy, Audie. *To Hell* 199-200

[264] Murphy, Audie *To Hell* 201

[265] Murphy, Edward F. 235

[266] McClure, David "How Audie Murphy won His Medals, Part V" *Audie Murphy Research Foundation Newsletter* Winter 1998-99 6

[267] McClure, David "How Audie Murphy won His Medals, Part V" 7

[268] reprinted from *Audie L. Murphy Memorial Website* www.audiemurphy.com

[269] Murphy, Audie. *To Hell* 208

[270] Murphy, Audie *To Hell* 214

[271] Murphy, Audie *To Hell* 215

[272] reprinted from *Audie L. Murphy Memorial Website* www.audiemurphy.com

[273] Murphy, Audie *Dallas Time Herald* article reprint 5

[274] Klein, Edward N. "Audie Murphy Did a Lot More Than Win a Bunch of Medals." *Hudson Valley Business Journal.* reprinted from *Audie L. Murphy Memorial Website* www.audiemurphy.com

[275] "Excerpts from July 1997 interview with Horace 'Red' Ditteriine" *Audie Murphy Research Foundation Newsletter* vol 2 Spring 1997 4

[276] "Interview with Charles L. Owens" *Audie Murphy Research Foundation Newsletter* vol 1 Winter 1997 3

[277] "Inside Story" *Entertainment Tonight* 1989

[278] Murphy, Audie *Dallas Times Herald* reprint 5

[279] Murphy, Audie *To Hell* 224

[280] Simpson 138

[281] Simpson 207

BOOK I Part 2 Chapter 6: Apotheosis

[282] Murphy, Edward F. 263

[283] Murphy, Edward F. 267

[284] Simpson 378

[285] "Interview with Charles L. Owens" *Audie Murphy Research Foundation Newsletter* Winter 1997 2

[286] Murphy, Audie. *To Hell* 241

[287] Reprinted from *Audie L. Murphy Memorial Website* www.audiemurphy.com

[288] Murphy, Audie *Dallas Times Herald* reprint 7

[289] Simpson 160

[290] Murphy, Audie <u>To Hell</u> 265-268

[291] "Interview with Charles L. Owens" *Research Foundation Audie Murphy Newsletter* Winter 1997 5

[292] Palumbo, Gene interview from *Audie Murphy Research Foundation Newsletter* Winter 1998 12

[293] Simpson 174

BOOK I Part 2 Chapter 7: The Granting of the Boon

[294] Campbell, Joseph. *Hero* 246

[295] Klein, Edward N. "Audie Murphy Did a Lot More Than Win a Bunch of Medals." *Hudson Valley Business Journal.* reprinted from *Audie L. Murphy Memorial Website* www.audiemurphy.com

[296] Butcher, Henry C. Captain, USNR *My Three Years with Eisenhower* (New York: Simon and Schuster 1946) 725, 732

[297] Butcher 743

[298] Butcher 770

[299] 401

[300] Murphy, Audie. *To Hell* 271

[301] Murphy, Audie *To Hell* 273

[302] Murphy, Audie *To Hell* 142

[303] Murphy, Audie "You Do the Prayin' and I'll Do the Shootin'." *Modern Screen* Jan 56 60

[304] Murphy, Audie *To Hell* 274

BOOK I Part 3: The Return

[305] Joseph Campbell *Hero with a Thousand Faces* 216

[306] Simpson, Harold. *Audie Murphy: American Soldier* (Dallas: Alcor Publishing Company 1982) 219

[307] Wilkie, Jane. "Memoirs of a Small Texan." *Modern Screen* July 1955 86

[308] Campbell, Joseph. *Hero with a Thousand Faces* (Princeton:Princeton University Press 1973) 193

[309] Campbell *Hero* 193

[310] Wilkie 86

[311] Simpson 222

[312] Simpson 222

[313] Simpson 223

[314] Morgan, Thomas B. "The War Hero." *Esquire* Dec 1983 602

[315] Simpson 224

[316] Simpson 226

[317] Simpson 227

[318] Simpson 224

[319] Simpson 229-230

[320] Schnurr, Paula P, Phd. "PTSD and Combat-Related Psychiatric Disorders in Older Veterans" *PTSD*

Research Quarterly Volume 2, Number 1 Winter 1991 2

[321] "PSTD and Older Veterans, A National Center for PTSD Fact Sheet National Center for Post-Traumatic Stress Disorder Web site www.ncptsd.va.gov

[322] "PTSD and Older Veterans"

[323] *DSM-IV Diagnostic and Statistical Manual of Mental Disorders* Fourth Edition (Washington, D. C.: American Psychiatric Association 1994)

[324] Herman 25

[325] Schnurr 2

[326] Schnurr 2

[327] Herman 25

[328] Formaini, Heather "Some Ideas about the Father's Body in Psychoanalytic Thought" *The C. G. Jung Page* www.cgjungpage.org

[329] *DSM-IV* 424

[330] Herman 36

[331] *DSM-IV* 425

[332] Herman 36

[333] *DSM-IV* 426

[334] Herman 49

[335] "Facts about Post-Traumatic Stress Disorder" *National Institute for Mental Health* Publication No. OM-99 4157 September 1999 1

[336] *DSM-IV* 426

[337] Herman 52

[338] Herman 54

[339] Herman 59

[340] "Excerpts from July 1997 Interview with Horace "Red" Dieterline" &" Part II: December 1996 Interview with Charles L. Owen" *Audie Murphy Research Foundation Newsletter* Spring 1997 3-6, 8-11

[341] "PTSD and Older Veterans"

[342] *DSM - IV* 427

[343] Herman 61

[344] Herman 61

[345] Schnurr 2

[346] *Audie Murphy Research Foundation Newsletter* Winter 1998 3

[347] Simpson 234

[348] Simpson 235

[349] Simpson 236

[350] Murphy, Audie *Dallas Times Herald* July 17 1945 reprinted in the *Audie Murphy Research Foundation Newsletter* Spring 1998 8

[351] Simpson 237

[352] Simpson 237

[353] Gossett 9

[354] Campbell *Hero* 217

BOOK II – Delivering the Message - Introduction

[355] Guches, Richard C. Ed. D "Psychological and Archetypal Analysis" *Sequel: A Handbook for the Critical analysis of Literature* (Palo Alto: Peek Publications) 1983 127

[356] McCurdy, Jole Cappriello "The Structural and Archetypal Analysis of Fairy Tales" *Psyche's Stories* Wilmette, Ill: Chiron Publications 1991 14

[357] Campbell, Joseph *Hero with a Thousand Faces* (Princeton: Princeton University Press) 1973 218

[358] Guches 127

[359] Campbell, Joseph *Hero with a Thousand Faces* (Princeton: University Press) 1973 36

[360] Campbell *Hero* 342

[361] Campbell *Hero* 345

[362] Pearson, Carol *Awakening the Heroes Within* (San Francisco: Harper) 1991 181

[363] Campbell *Hero* 347

[364] Campbell *Hero* 349

[365] Campbell *Hero* 354

[366] Pearson, Carol *The Hero Within* (San Francisco: Harper 1989) 98

BOOK II Chapter 1: Stranger in a Strange Land

[367] Arnold, Maxine "The Personal War of Audie Murphy" *Photoplay* Oct 1955 108

[368] Hubler, Richard. "He Doesn't Want to be a Star." *Saturday Evening Post* 18 April 1953 155

[369] Hubler 155

[370] Simpson, Harold. *Audie Murphy: American Soldier* (Dallas: Alcor Publishing Company 1982) 347

[371] Holliday, Kate "Still in Stride" *Screenland* April 1949 64

[372] Holliday 65

[373] Holliday 65

[374] Hubler 155

[375] quoted in Simpson 260

[376] quoted in Simpson 258

[377] Simpson 258

[378] Simpson 258

[379] McClure, David "Audie Murphy: the Man" unpublished manuscript

[380] Simpson 259

[381] Simpson 257

[382] Simpson 22

[383] "Audie Murphy: Great American Hero"

[384] "James Cagney Biography" from *Baseline's Encyclopedia of Film*, Cinemania Microsoft Corp. 1993

[385] Hubler 155

[386] Simpson 259

[387] "James Cagney Biography"

[388] Hubler 155

[389] Arnold 108

[390] Holliday 64

[391] McClure, David "Audie Murphy: The Man"

[392] Herman, Judith M. D. *Trauma and Recovery* (New York: Basic Books 1997) 155

[393] Herman 162

[394] Hubler 153

[395] Simpson 264

[396] Morgan, Thomas B. "The War Hero." *Esquire* Dec 1983 602

[397] Simpson 264

[398] Arnold 62-63

[399] McClure, David "How Audie Murphy Became a Movie Star" *Movieland* 1955 Quoted in Simpson 258

[400] *Audie Murphy Research Foundation Newsletter* Winter 1998 3

[401] Arnold 108

[402] Hubler 155

[403] Simpson 363

[404] Murphy, Audie *To Hell* 125

[405] Arnold 108

[406] Simpson 203

[407] Simpson 259

[408] Simpson 266

[409] Simpson 347

[410] Hubler 155

[411] Moore, Viola "They're Doing All They Can" *Motion Picture* April 1950 67

[412] Simpson 270

BOOK II Chapter 2: The Bad Boy of Hollywood

[413] The account of Murphy's brother's placement at Boy's Ranch and of Murphy's subsequent role in "Bad Boy" is adapted from an entry to the "Movies of Audie Murphy" page of the Audie L. Murphy Memorial Website, www.audiemurphy.com, with the permission of webmaster Richard Rodgers.

[414] Holliday, Kate. "Still is Stride. *Screenland* April 49 65

[415] Hubler, Richard. "He Doesn't Want to be a Star." *Saturday Evening Post* 18 April 1953 35

[416] Hubler 158

[417] Hubler 157

[418] Simpson 268

[419] Simpson 261

[420] Simpson n265

[421] Arnold 108

[422] Arnold 63

[423] Simpson 347

[424] "Audie Murphy: Great American Hero" *A&E Biography*

[425] Simpson

[426] "Audie Murphy: Great American Hero"

BOOK II Chapter 3 Master of Two Worlds

[427] "Korean War" *Compton's Concise Encyclopedia* 1995 Compton's NewMedia, Inc.

[428] Simpson Harold. *Audie Murphy: American Soldier* (Dallas: Alcor Publishing Company 1982) 339

[429] "Korean War"

[430] Simpson 341

[431] "Korean War"

[432] Simpson 343

[433] "Korean War"

[434] Simpson 269

[435] "Testimony of Audie Murphy" *Illicit Narcotics Traffic (Washington, D. C): Hearings before the Subcommittee on Improvements in the Federal Criminal Code of the Committee of the Juciciary, United States Sentate* (Washington: GPO 1956)906

[436] See "The Last Real Action Hero," later in this work

[437] Simpson 343

[438] Campbell, Joseph. *Hero with a Thousand Faces* (Princeton: Princeton University Press 1977) 229

[439] Campbell, Joseph. *The Power of Myth* (New York: Anchor Books 1988) 46

[440] Matheson, Richard "The Enemy Within" *Star Trek* Paramount 1966

[441] Simpson 271

[442] Simpson 370

[443] Simpson 369

[444] Simpson 351

[445] Squire, Charles. *Celtic Myth and Legend* (Van Nuys: Newcastle Publishing Company 1975) 159

BOOK II Chapter 4: From Duel to Destry

[446] Foulke, Robert and Smith, Paul "The Romance" *Elements of Literature, Sixth Course: The Literature of Britain* (New York: Holt, Rinehart, and Winston) 1991

[447] Tuska, John. *The American West in Film* (Westport, Conn: Greenwood Press 1995) 17

[448] Pearson, Carol *The Hero Within* (San Francisco: HarperColllins Publishers) 1989 151

[449] Campbell, Joseph. *The Masks of God:Creative Mythology* (New York: Penguin Books 1987) 461

[450] Squire, Charles. *Celtic Myth and Legend* (Van Nuys: Newcastle Publishing Company 1975) 369

[451] Hutchings, Peter, "Genre theory and criticism," ed. Hollows, Joan and Jancovich, Mark. *Approaches to Popular Film* (New York: Manchester University Press 1995) 62

[452] Hutchings, Peter 69

[453] May, Rollo *The Cry for Myth* (New York: Dell Publishing Company) 1991 96-98

[454] Campbell, Joseph. *Flight of the Wild Gander* New York: Harper Perennial 1990) 222

[455] Foulke and Smith

[456] Guches, Richard "Psychological and Archetypal Analysis" *Sequel: A Handbook for the Critical*

Analysis of Literature (Palo Alto: Peek Publications 1985) 132-134

[457] Pearson 151

[458] Simpson, Harold *Audie Murphy: American Hero* (Dallas: Alcor Publishing 1982) 286

[459] Gossett, Sue *The Films and Careers of Audie Murphy* Madison, N. C: Empire Publishing, Inc 1997)

[460] Campbell *Hero* 342

[461] "Gunsmoke" dir. Nathan Juran Audie Murphy, Susan Cabot, Paul Kelly, Jack Kelly Universal-International 1953

[462] Clooney, Nick. "Matinee Classics" American Movie Classics July 1996

[463] Clooney

[464] Allen, William. *Anzio: Edge of Disaster* (New York: Elsevier-Dutton Publishing Company 1978) 40

[465] Clooney

[466] Gossett *52*

[467] Campbell, Joseph. *Hero with a Thousand Faces* (Princeton: Princeton University Press 1977) 246

[468] Gossett 56

[469] Simpson 268

[470] Dorian, Bob. "Bob Dorian's Classic Hollywood. *American Movie Classics Magazine* June 1997 12

[471] Gossett 65

[472] "Destry" dir. George Marshall, Audie Murphy, Mari Blanchard, Lyle Bettger, Thomas Mitchell Universal-International 1954

[473] Hubler, Richard, "He Doesn't Want to be a Star," *Saturday Evening Post* 18 April 1953 35

[474] Morgan, Thomas B. "The War Hero" *Esquire* December 1983

[475] *Audie Murphy Research Foundation Newsletter* various articles from 1997 through 1998

BOOK II Chapter 5: Reliving Hell

[476] Hubler, Richard. "He Doesn't Want to be a Star." *Saturday Evening Post* 18 April 1953 155

[477] Gossett, Sue. *The Films and Career of Audie Murphy* (Madison, N.C: Empire Publishing, Inc 1997) 69

[478] Scott, John L. "Audie Murphy, No. 1 Hero, Slogs Again." *Los Angeles Times* September, 1955

[479] Simpson 271

[480] Simpson 271

[481] "The Man Who Lived Twice." *Screen Album* May-July 1956

[482] "Murphy Will Appear for Opening of Hell" *Dallas Times Herald* August 14, 1955

[483] Gossett 70

[484] Gossett 70

[485] Gossett 70

[486] Scott 2

[487] Simpson 271

[488] Simpson 275

[489] Gossett 70

[490] Simpson 275

BOOK II Chapter 6: Fatherhood

[491] Campbell, Joseph *Hero with a Thousand Faces* (Princeton: Princeton University Press 1977) 345

[492] Pearson, Carol *Awakening the Heroes Within* (San Francisco: Harper 1991) 161

[493] Guches, Richard C. Ed. D "Psychological and Archetypal Analysis" *Sequel: A Handbook for the Critical Analysis of Literature* (Palo Alto: Peek Publications 1983) 127

[494] Simpson, Harold. *Audie Murphy: American Soldier* (Dallas: Alcor Publishing Company 1982) 286

[495] "The Man Who Lived Twice," *Screen Album* May-July 1956

[496] Simpson 286

[497] Campbell. *Hero* 347

[498] Simpson 270

[499] Arnold, Maxine "The Personal War of Audie Murphy *Photoplay* October 1955 62

[500] Chodorow, Nancy *Feminism and Psychoanalytic Theory* (New York: Yale University Press 1989) 32

[501] "Rancher Audie Murphy" *TV Radio Mirror* June 1961 45

[502] Hubler 158

[503] Formaini, Heather "Some Ideas about the Father's Body in Psychoanalytic Thought" *The C. G. Jung Page* www.cgjungpage.org (italics added)

[504] Morgan, Thomas B. "The War Hero." *Esquire* Dec 1983 603

[505] Campbell. *Hero* 349

[506] Campbell *Hero* 238

[507] Gossett, Sue *The Films and Career of Audie Murphy* Madison, N. C: Empire Publishing Company 1997) 163

BOOK II Chapter 7: The Freedom to Live

[508] Campbell, Joseph *Hero with a Thousand Faces* (Princeton University Press 1973) 238

[509] Campbell 238

[510] "PTSD and Older Veterans, A National Center for PTSD Fact Sheet National Center for Post-Traumatic Stress Disorder www.ncptsd.va.gov

[511] Campbell *Hero* 239

[512] Simpson, Harold *Audie Murphy: American Soldier* (Dallas: Alcor Publishing Company 1982) 278

[513] Gossett, Sue *The Films and Career of Audie Murphy* (Madison, N. C.: Empire Publishing Company 1977)

[514] Gossett 73

[515] "World in My Corner" dir. Jesse Hibbs Audie Murphy, Barbara Rush, Jeff Morrow, John McIntire Universal-International 1955

[516] Thomas, Tony. *The Best of Universal* (New York: Vestal Press, Ltd. 1990) 39

[517] Gossett 76

[518] "Behind the Scenes with 'Walk the Proud Land'." *Screen Stories* Oct 1956 48

[519] Gossett 79

[520] Tuska, John *The American West in Film* (Westport: Greenwood Press 1985) 253

[521] Simpson 277

[522] Clooney, Nick "Matinee Classics" *American Movie Classics* March 28 1999

[523] Simpson 277

[524] Gossett 86

[525] Clooney, Nick "Matinee Classics" *American Movie Classics*

[526] Jung, Carl *Man and His Symbols* (New York: Dell Publishing Company 1968) 73

[527] Campbell, Joseph *Hero* 38

[528] Greene, Graham *The Quiet American: Text and Criticism* ed. John Clark Pratt (New York: Penguin Books 1996)

[529] Gossett 90

[530] Larryann Willis, Executive Director, Audie Murphy Research Foundation from a comment on the Biography message board www.biography.com August 17, 1998

[531] Willis www.biography.com August 19, 1998

[532] Greene 94

[533] McClure, David "Audie Murphy: Man of Humor."

[534] Gossett 112

[535] Ehle, John *Trail of Tears: The Rise and Fall of the Cherokee Nation* (New York: Anchor Books 1988)

[536] "The Wild and the Innocent" dir. Jack Sher Audie Murphy, Joanne Dru, Gilbert Roland, Sandra Dee Universal-International 1959

[537] Gossett 112

[538] "Inside Story" *Entertainment Tonight* 1959

BOOK II Chapter 8: Songwriter

[539] Gossett, Sue *The Films and Career of Audie Murphy* (Madison, N. C: Empire Publishing Company 1997) 183

[540] Simpson, Harold *Audie Murphy" American Soldier* (Dallas: Alcor Publishing Company 1982) 376

[541] Simpson 373

[542] Posted by Larryann Willis, Executive Director, Audie Murphy Research Foundation, at www.biography.com August 18 1998 (printed here with permission of the Audie Murphy Research Foundation)

BOOK II Chapter 9: The Last Real Action Hero

[543] "Universal Pictures" *Baseline's Encyclopedia of Film*, Cinemania Microsoft Corp.1993

[544] Simpson, Harold *Audie Murphy: American Soldier* (Dallas: Alcor Publishing Company 1982)

[545] Gossett, Sue. *The Films and Career of Audie Murphy* (Madison, N. C: Empire Publishing Company 1997) 173

[546] Simpson 278

[547] Gossett 174

[548] Gossett 176

[549] May, Rollo *The Cry for Myth* (New York: Delta 1991) 56

[550] May 100

[551] Simpson 278

[552] Morgan 603

[553] Simpson 280

[554] Fishburn, Jay quoted from *Audie Murphy Research Foundation Newsletter* vol 2 Spring 1997

[555] Morgan 603

[556] Simpson 413

[557] Simpson 413

[558] Campbell, Joseph *Hero with a Thousand Faces* (Princeton: Princeton University Press 1973) 355

[559] Jung, Emma and von Franz, Marie Louise *The Grail Legend* (Boston: Sigo Books 1980) 384

[560] Campbell, Joseph *Hero 358*

[561] Simpson 322

[562] Simpson 288

[563] "To Hell and Not Quite Back" *Time* 14 July 1971 27

[564] Simpson 279

[565] Simpson 388

BOOK II Chapter 10: Departure

[566] May 115.

[567] Campbell, Joseph, *Hero with a Thousand Faces* (Princeton: Princeton University Press 1973) 319

[568] "PSTD and Older Veterans, A National Center for PTSD Fact Sheet National Center for Post-Traumatic Stress Disorder Web site www.ncptsd.va.gov

[569] Fishburn, Jay quoted from *Audie Murphy Research Foundation Newsletter* vol 2 Spring 1997

Made in the USA
San Bernardino, CA
29 July 2013